VGM Opportunities Series

OPPORTUNITIES IN
PHYSICIAN CAREERS

Jan Sugar-Webb

Revised by
Julie Rigby

VGM Career Horizons
NTC/Contemporary Publishing Group

Library of Congress Cataloging-in-Publication Data

Sugar-Webb, Jan, 1954-
      Opportunities in physician careers / Jan Sugar-Webb ; revised by
Julie Rigby.
            p.   cm. — (VGM opportunities series)
            ISBN 0-8442-2979-2 (cloth). — ISBN 0-8442-2984-9 (pbk.)
            1. Medicine—Specialties and specialists.   2. Medicine—Vocational
      guidance.   I. Rigby, Julie.   II. Title.   III. Series.
      R729.5.S6S84   1999
      610.69—dc21   99-33038
                                                                                         CIP

Cover photographs: © PhotoDisc, Inc.

Published by VGM Career Horizons
A division of NTC/ Contemporary Publishing Group, Inc.
4255 West Touhy Avenue, Lincolnwood (Chicago), Illinois 60712-1975 U.S.A.

International Standard Book Number: 0-8442-2979-2 (cloth)
                                                    0-8442-2984-9 (paper)
   00 01 02 03 04 LB 18 17 16 15 14 13 12 11 10 9   8   7   6   5   4   3   2

CONTENTS

Ancient Egyptians. Hippocrates and the influence of Greek medicine. The Renaissance. The seventeenth century—greater understanding. The eighteenth century—the beginning of prevention. The nineteenth century and the rise of modern medicine. The twentieth century—revolutionary progress. The future of medicine.

Getting into medical school. Medical school today.

Residents, interns, and fellows. Specialization. Certification. Location of residency programs. Hours worked. Financing residency training. New trends in graduate medical education.

Family practice. Internal medicine.

ABOUT THE AUTHOR

Jan Sugar-Webb, M.A., is an award-winning communications and marketing consultant in Chicago. Through her communications firm, Sugar-Webb & Associates, she frequently works with health care organizations and physicians. She is a former director of public affairs at Mount Sinai Hospital on Chicago's West Side. Prior to that appointment, she was a research and policy writer for the American Medical Association, where she worked on the "Health Policy Agenda for the American People," the AMA's blueprint for the delivery of health care in the twenty-first century.

Ms. Sugar-Webb holds a bachelor's degree in literature from Simmons College in Boston and a master's degree in education from Boston University. Her broad experience as a teacher includes directing a program for high school dropouts from the inner city and implementing a training program for teachers of the disabled at City Colleges of Chicago.

Julie Rigby is a writer and editor living in Vermont.

FOREWORD

The decision to enter the medical profession is an important and life-changing event. Many people choose to study and practice medicine because they are drawn to the excitement and challenges that come with being a doctor. They thrive on the high-pressure work, where life and death decisions must sometimes be made in a matter of minutes. And they welcome the intellectual, physical, and emotional challenges of a demanding job. For many future physicians, the decision to pursue this career is motivated by a calling to work in a field that really makes a difference in other peoples' lives, where the rewards of helping others by relieving their pain and suffering is even more important than the excellent salary opportunities and the prestige associated with being a doctor.

Now more than ever, those drawn to a career in medicine face an astonishing array of possibilities. Medical students can choose from dozens of medical specialties and subspecialties and a wide range of environments in which to work. They may elect to work in small or large hospitals, research laboratories, private practice, or overseas with underprivileged or mobile populations. They may focus specifically on helping children, women, the aged, or populations here and abroad affected by AIDS and other medical crises.

Whatever area of medicine you choose to work in, you can be assured that this field will demand your best. The grueling medical school preparation, followed by intensive hands-on residency training, will test your limits and strengthen your character. Medicine is truly a field that calls for the best and brightest of our population. The challenges facing the medical profession are numerous, the need for qualified, caring physicians is constant, and the opportunities are there for all.

The Editors
VGM Career Books

CHAPTER 1

PHYSICIANS—A HISTORICAL PERSPECTIVE

Throughout human history, people have turned to special practitioners who know how to promote greater health and relieve pain and suffering. From the earliest spiritual healers to today's experts in the latest medical techniques, the history of medicine reflects the integral role played by physicians.

Our ancient ancestors believed that spirits were the cause of death and disease. Illness was thought to arise when a spirit invaded the body. They believed that pain was connected to forces at work in the world that were beyond the control of humankind. In the cosmic view of primitive peoples, a web of mystical processes was responsible for natural occurrences. They believed that rain, fire, fertility, and agriculture were all dependent on the goodwill of unseen gods and spirits. Health could only be obtained by following the whims and rules of these spirits. For that reason, the earliest "doctors" were in fact sorcerers of a sort, people who could communicate with and ward off malevolent spirits.

At the Cave of the Three Brothers in France, explorers found what is likely the oldest picture of a healer. In the painting, done on a wall in the cave perhaps twenty-five thousand years ago, the figure is dancing; he has human feet but the paws of a bear. Antlers sprout out of his head. His eyes stare outward. It is believed that this person is a tribal doctor, wrapped in animal skins, driving evil spirits away. His ability to do magic gives him the power to heal the sick.

ANCIENT EGYPTIANS

Archaeologists working at ancient sites of human habitation have found evidence that our ancestors used herb therapies and even primitive surgery to heal the sick. Perhaps the most skillful and advanced medical practices of the ancient world can be found in Egypt.

Ancient Egyptians believed in immortality, that the soul would return to the body sometime after death. Egyptians preserved the bodies of the dead along with treasured possessions. They documented events on writing material called papyrus. The medical papyri of Egyptian physicians describe the ways they treated ailments and reveal a detailed knowledge of anatomy.

Although the Egyptians had a relatively advanced understanding of the human body, their medical practices still involved magic. The believed that many diseases were caused by wormlike creatures that invaded the body. Physicians and magicians would work together, combining medicines and spells to treat everything from scorpion stings to snake bites.

The most famous and detailed medical papyri are named after the men who obtained them in Egypt and shared them with the world—Smith and Ebers. The Smith papyrus outlines forty-eight surgical cases, including diagnoses and methods of treatment. It deals exclusively with wounds and fractures. The treatment offered for the cases is mostly practical but suggests a mix of magical incantations and remedies, including one "to change an old man into a youth of twenty."

The Smith papyrus is an impressive document. The author of the original papyrus was probably a gifted surgeon who used practical interventions, like the following recommendation for treating a fractured collarbone:

> You must lay him down outstretched on his back, with something folded between his two shoulder blades. Then you must spread his two shoulder blades so that his two collarbones stretch, so that the fracture falls into its proper place. Then you must make him two compresses of cloth. Then you must place one of them inside his upper arm, the other below his upper arm...

Some of the recommended treatments are still used today. When the ailing patient has a dislocated jaw, the doctor is instructed to put his thumbs inside the patient's mouth. The doctor's other fingers go under the patient's chin, and the doctor guides the jaw back into its proper place. This treatment is still the only treatment used for a dislocated jaw.

The Ebers papyrus, which was probably composed around 2000 B.C., is mostly a text on internal medicine. It names diseases and remedies as well as some cosmetic aids. Like the Smith papyrus, parts of the Ebers papyrus contain observant medical data:

> If you examine a person who suffers from pains in the stomach and is sick in the arm, the breast, and the stomach, and it appears that it is the disease uat, you will say: 'Death has entered into the mouth and has taken its seat there.' You will prepare a remedy composed of the following plants: the stalks of the plant tehus, mint, the red seeds of the plant sechet; and you will have them cooked in beer; you will give it to the sick person and his arm will be easily extended without pain, and then you will say, 'The disease has gone out from the intestine through the anus, it is not necessary to repeat the medicine.'

The Ebers papyrus also contains more magical treatments for diseases, like a frog warmed in oil for a burn. (This treatment is to be accompanied by a chant.)

Although contributions to medicine came from many eras in history and many places in the world, the Greeks have had the greatest influence on modern Western medicine. Nowhere in Homer's *Iliad,* written between 900 and 800 B.C., does he mention any incantations to treat the wounds of war. Instead, Homer writes of treatments that were strictly medical.

HIPPOCRATES AND THE INFLUENCE
OF GREEK MEDICINE

The most famous of the Greek physicians was Hippocrates, who is known as the "father of medicine." Hippocrates was born around 460 B.C. on the island of Cos, where he founded a school of medicine. His teachings, which included careful, detailed observation of the patient, encouraged the separation of medicine and religion and gave a scientific and moral basis to medicine. Hippocrates wrote:

> In acute diseases the physician must make his observations in the following way. He must first look at the face of the patient and see whether it is like that of people in good health, and, particularly, whether it is like its usual self, for this is the best of all; whereas the most opposite to it is the worst, such as the following; nose sharp, eyes hollow, temples sunken, ears cold and contracted and their lobes turned out, and the skin about the face dry, tense, and parched, the color of the face as a whole being yellow or black, livid or lead colored...

Hippocrates also taught that wounds should be washed in boiled water and that doctors' hands should be clean. Many of the observations that Hippocrates and his pupils made about the human body are still valid in terms of modern Western medicine. He wrote:

> When sleep puts an end to delirium it is a good sign.
> Weariness without cause indicates disease.
> If there be a painful affection in any part of the body,
> but no suffering, there is mental disorder.

Hippocrates also had a moral vision of what a physician should be—a professional assisting in the healing process in every way. His oath is still taken by graduating medical students today.

Hippocratic medicine was carried on in the Egyptian medical school founded by two Greeks, Herophilus and Erasistratus. They dissected human bodies and learned about how the organs worked. The Greeks also developed Roman medicine. The Greek physician Galen, who was born in A.D. 130, became the most famous and influential physician in Rome. His writings on anatomy and physiology were held as the standard medical authority for centuries.

THE RENAISSANCE

With the dissolution of the Roman Empire in around A.D. 400, the development of modern Western medicine was stifled for several centuries. It surged forward again after the eighth century, when the Arabs spread their empire from the Middle East to Spain, founding new medical schools and hospitals.

By the beginning of the Renaissance several centuries later, new interest was aroused in medicine. During the fifteenth century, the Renaissance was at its pinnacle, and medicine was even studied and advanced by artists like Leonardo da Vinci who made careful drawings of the structure of the human body. Andreas Vesalius's book, *Fabric of the Human Body,* was published in 1543. As the first real written anatomy of the human body, this work promoted the practice of surgery throughout the world.

THE SEVENTEENTH CENTURY— GREATER UNDERSTANDING

During the seventeenth century, three major contributions to medicine were made. In 1628 William Harvey, an English physician, published *De Motu Cordis et Sanguinis in Animalibus.* In it he describes his discovery of how blood circulates in the body. It has remained one of the most famous medical texts ever written both because of its enthusiastic style and because it outlines one of the most important medical discoveries ever made. Harvey also developed the study of nutrition to improve the health of the general public.

Later in the century, an Italian histologist named Marcello Malpighi filled the gap left in Harvey's discoveries by creating the first description of the capillaries that connect arteries and veins.

The Dutch scientist Anthony van Leeuwenhoek refined the microscope. He used home-ground lenses with short focal lengths to observe what could not be seen before, such as red corpuscles, spermatozoa, and bacteria.

THE EIGHTEENTH CENTURY— THE BEGINNING OF PREVENTION

By the eighteenth century, much was known about the workings of the human body. This century was primarily a time of systematization and classification. Carl von Linné (or Linnaeus), the Swedish botanist and physician, established the idea of classification both in botany and in medicine. He was the originator of the binomial nomenclature in science, classifying each natural object by a family name and a specific name, like homo sapiens for humans.

The eighteenth century witnessed great strides in the development of preventive medicine. Sanitation improved as sewers were covered and streets were paved. In 1796, Edward Jenner developed the first vaccine against smallpox. For years, smallpox epidemics had wreaked havoc with the population, killing many. When the smallpox vaccine was given to 12,000 people in London, the yearly rate of the disease dropped from 2,018 to 622.

Other important medical advances were made by Caspar Wolff and John Hunter. Caspar Friedrich Wolff, a German, is noted for his major contribution to modern embryology.

Wolff noted that the embryo was not preformed and encased in the ovary, as previously believed, but rather that organs are formed "in leaf-like layers." John Hunter, a Scottish surgeon who practiced in London, was an influential physician and teacher who helped win respect for surgery as a scientific profession.

THE NINETEENTH CENTURY AND
THE RISE OF MODERN MEDICINE

Modern medicine as we know it began during the nineteenth century. The causes of many diseases were beginning to be identified, and effective treatments were being developed. The nineteenth century also brought advances in medical research and the birth of modern surgery.

One key discovery occurred when a French physician, Jean Corvisart des Marets, found that certain parts of the body give different sounds when thumped. The sound changes if fluid is present. This important diagnostic tool is called *percussing.*

Another French physician, Réné-Théophile-Hyacinthe Laennec, invented the stethoscope in 1819. It is said that he found percussing the chest of one of his patients too difficult, so he rolled up a cylinder of paper in his hands and placed it against the patient's chest to listen. His publication of successive editions of *Traité de l'auscultation médiate* became the foundation of modern knowledge of diseases of the chest and their diagnosis.

And in 1846 at Massachusetts General Hospital in Boston modern surgery was born when William Morton first anesthetized a patient with ether. Unfortunately, patients continued to die on the operating table from infection until the chemist Louis Pasteur's discovery that bacteria caused disease was taken seriously.

The Scottish surgeon, Joseph Lister, understood the importance of Pasteur's discovery. Lister first tried to kill the bacteria that entered his patients during surgery. Later, he tried to prevent bacteria from entering wounds by boiling instruments and using antiseptic solutions. Also building on Pasteur's work, a German physician named Robert Koch experimented with his bacteria. He identified the germ that causes tuberculosis and developed the science of bacteriology.

As the causes of disease were becoming more familiar, research into the prevention of disease flourished. The Russian bacteriologist Elie Metchnikoff discovered that certain white blood cells attack bacteria and other particles that enter the blood. And in 1890 Karl Landsteiner, a German surgeon, discovered a cure for diphtheria. Landsteiner discovered the four main blood types and made blood transfusion possible for the first time. That same year, Emil von Behring and Shibasabura developed vaccines against tetanus and diphtheria.

THE TWENTIETH CENTURY—
REVOLUTIONARY PROGRESS

The twentieth century has seen a tremendous explosion in the understanding and treatment of diseases. Foremost among the developments is an increasingly sophisticated knowledge of how to prevent the onset and spread of illness. As well, the technological advances of this century moved medical practice forward by leaps and bounds. In the early 1900s, Wilhelm Roentgen began applying his technique of x-rays to medicine. This radical new discovery allowed doctors to diagnose problems that previously had been invisible to them and advanced surgery as a science.

Another breakthrough came with the discovery of penicillin in 1928. In England, Sir Alexander Fleming discovered by chance that staphylococcus actually dissolved when exposed to *Penicillium notatum*. Fleming extracted an active principle that he called "penicillin," which was superb in treating infection. Penicillin was eventually mass produced in the 1940s and has saved millions of lives. And with the introduction of the BCG vaccine and streptomycin, tuberculosis, which had been the leading cause of death in the developed world, was nearly eradicated.

Following World War II, medical research increased exponentially. Jonas Salk's polio vaccine was part of the revolutionary developments in pharmacological medicine of the 1950s and changed the face of childhood, both at home and abroad. Other drug breakthroughs of the era, such as steroids like cortisone and immunosuppressants, made it possible for doctors to tackle illnesses of the immune system and opened up the possibilities for plastic and transplant surgeries. Open-heart surgery became possible in the 1950s; another leap forward, bypass operations, began in 1967. That very year Christiaan Barnard implanted a women's heart into a man, who then lived for eighteen days. By the end of the twentieth century, hundreds of heart transplant surgeries were being performed every year, and patients were living five years or longer with their donor hearts.

The twentieth century was also a period of unprecedented technical advances. The development of electron microscopes, endoscopes, computerized axial tomography (CAT), lasers, and other diagnostic tools radically transformed the practice of medicine. Discoveries in genetic and molecular biology, such as Francis Crick and James Watson's cracking of the genetic code in 1953, also moved medicine in a new direction.

In 1979 the world was declared free of smallpox, and in 1994 the United States was declared a polio-free zone. By the end of the century, it was hard to imagine a time before mammographies became routine and many forms of cancer were able to be treated with drugs, surgery, and chemotherapy.

THE FUTURE OF MEDICINE

The monumental strides of the twentieth century have helped increase life span and have fundamentally altered the way people look at health and illness. Never before have we lived so well, for so long. Where people once commonly died from polio, diphtheria, and smallpox, modern medicine now allows us to survive illnesses and accidents that would have been devastating before.

The twenty-first century promises to be an era of even greater medical expansion. For those who enter the medical profession, medicine in the future will not only give them more tools to help their patients, it will also raise challenging ethical issues. Questions regarding such issues as medical euthanasia, surrogate parenting, and the equitable distribution of medical resources will influence medical practice. New strains of diseases will need to be cured, and the battle against AIDS has yet to be won.

The opportunities in medicine are endless, and the need for doctors who are committed to helping others—the rich and the poor, at home and abroad—has never been greater.

CHAPTER 2

EDUCATION AND PREPARATION

One hundred and fifty years ago, becoming a doctor was considerably less complicated than it is today. Medical school lasted less than a year, and the M.D. degree was conferred regardless of grades. Although the minimum age requirement for becoming a doctor was twenty-one, this rule was not strictly followed. Instead of intensive laboratory and clinical preparation, students learned solely by attending lectures. In fact, the medical schools of the era were called proprietary schools, because the lecturers who instructed the students (usually fewer than a dozen) often owned the schools themselves.

The face of medical education changed in the mid-nineteenth century, as American doctors began to travel more extensively in Europe, where they were exposed to the new laboratory methods being developed by European doctors. At the same time, the modern university was emerging, and new regulatory authority was being assumed by state and federal governments. By 1910, when Abraham Flexner published his famous report that outlined the conditions in American and Canadian medical schools, the foundation for modern medical education was well under way.

With the growth of medical knowledge, research and teaching became full-time activities for some in the medical profession. By the late nineteenth century, the academic physician was very prominent. As we enter the twenty-first century, the division between academic and clinical medicine still exists. And the development of the medical scholar has had an enduring impact on the way medical schools now operate.

GETTING INTO MEDICAL SCHOOL

Admission to medical school is extremely competitive. In the late 1990s, there were about 43,000 applicants for the 16,200 available spots at the 127 medical schools in the United States. Thus, your chances of getting into medical school—any medical school—is less than 50 percent.

Most applicants naturally want to attend what they consider the "best" medical schools. There are of course many factors that influence the ratings of medical schools, such as class size, location, clinical facilities, and other resources. Given that, it is extremely difficult to reliably rate which schools are the best, although the schools listed below are generally considered among the most prestigious. For that reason, admissions at these schools are even more competitive than elsewhere.

Albert Einstein College of Medicine
Baylor College of Medicine
Columbia University College of Physicians and Surgeons
Cornell University Medical College
Duke University School of Medicine
Harvard Medical School
Johns Hopkins University School of Medicine
New York University School of Medicine
Stanford University School of Medicine
University of California, Los Angeles
University of California, San Diego
University of California, San Francisco
University of Chicago, Pritzker School of Medicine
University of Michigan Medical School
University of Minnesota, Minneapolis
University of Pennsylvania School of Medicine
University of Texas, Dallas
Vanderbilt University School of Medicine
Washington University School of Medicine
Yale University School of Medicine

Most applicants apply to an average of fifteen schools. You will have a better chance of being accepted if you carefully research and choose the schools to which you apply. The more you know about the process of applying to medical school, the better your chances of finding your place in the medical profession.

During High School

Some doctors know from a very young age that medicine will be their future path. While still in high school, they take their first steps down this road.

It makes sense early on to find out you like or can handle the rigorous premedical courses necessary to get into medical school. You might try taking a few difficult science courses while still in high school.

Even more important is finding ways to gain early exposure to the medical field. Whether you find a paid job in a lab during the summer or a volunteer position working in a hospice, you can learn a lot by being involved in the medical field before college. When you apply to medical school, these experiences will make you a more attractive candidate to admissions committees.

Good grades and good study habits are important elements for preparing for a future in medicine. Medical school is a long and arduous process that takes more hard work and hours than perhaps any other profession. Early training in intense studying is an asset.

If you are sure while you are still in high school that you want to go to medical school, you might consider combining your undergraduate and medical studies. Many of the programs are six years long. Others take seven and eight years to complete. The programs avoid the medical school application process and let students take courses they would naturally pick without the constant worry about getting into medical school. The list of universities and colleges that have combined programs is found in Appendix B at the back of the book.

Grade Point Average in College

It shouldn't surprise you to learn that your college grade point average is very important to the admissions officers at medical schools. They will look at both your science grade point average, as well as your overall grade point average. Your chances of getting into the medical school of your choice increase with your grades. In recent years, the mean grade point average of accepted applicants has been just over 3.4 (out of 4.0). Nearly 50 percent of applicants had a GPA of 3.5 or above, while only 2 percent of students with a GPA under 2.5 were accepted to medical school. Medical schools will allow for certain special factors if you have a less than stellar GPA, for example, if you come from an educationally disadvantaged background. Nevertheless, you should strive for the highest grades possible, as improvement in upper-class years can also work in your favor.

Medical College Admissions Test

The Medical College Admissions Test (MCAT) is a multiple-choice, standardized exam administered by the American Association of Medical Colleges (AAMC). The test measures proficiency in the basic sciences, as well as general problem-solving, critical thinking, and communications skills. The MCAT is a very important selection factor for admission into medical school.

The test is given twice a year, in April and in August. Most medical schools suggest that potential applicants take the MCAT in the spring of the year they are applying. The MCAT consists of four timed sections, including breaks, administered over a period of more than seven hours.

The four sections, the number of questions in each section, and the amount of time they take are shown below:

Section	Questions	Time (in minutes)
Verbal reasoning	65	85
Physical science	77	100
Essay writing	2	60
Biological sciences	77	100

The four sections of the MCAT are scored separately. The two essays, which measure written communication skills, are assigned a letter grade of J (lowest) to T (highest). The physical sciences, biological sciences, and verbal reasoning sections are scored on a scale of 1 (lowest) to 15 (highest). A score of between 8 and 10 on these sections is considered superior.

On the day you arrive to take the MCAT, you will be offered the "Score Choice" option. This special option allows you to see your MCAT scores before they are released to the medical schools that you are applying to. Then, if you are not happy with your scores, you can elect to retake the test and have your new scores sent to the medical schools. However, even if schools only receive your new scores, they will still be able to tell that you have taken the MCAT twice.

There is a wide range of review courses and practice books available to help you prepare for the MCAT. You also can receive a student manual directly from the MCAT, which contains sample questions. How much time you prepare for the MCAT is up to you, although some people suggest that you begin up to nine months before you take the test. It is important not only to know your material and answer the questions correctly, but to do it in as little time as possible. With enough practice, however, you can become more adept at taking the test within the limited time allowed.

Undergraduate Course Work

Not that long ago, you almost had to be a science major if you wanted to go to medical school. Undergraduates used to concentrate on typical "premed" files like biology, chemistry, and physics.

Now medical schools look for students who have a broad, liberal arts education. Admissions officers are interested in applicants who have strong intellectual and communications skills, as well as a strong foundation in the sciences. Naturally, medical school is science-intensive, and it is important that you are able to handle the heavy course work.

Although course requirements vary from school to school, general requirements are one year each of biology or zoology, inorganic chemistry, organic chemistry, physics, and English. The science courses should be rigorous and include sufficient laboratory experience.

Many medical schools also require or recommend calculus or college-level math courses. A few of the more prestigious medical schools also require advanced-level science courses.

Applying to Medical School

The application process to medical school is fraught with hope and fear for most students. Since gaining entrance is a combination of good grades and MCAT scores, recommendations, extracurricular activities, and your personal essay, it is no wonder that the process is a dizzying experience. There are so many variables that you can never be sure of the outcome.

The value of good grades and MCAT scores was mentioned earlier in the chapter. The following is a brief explanation of the other parts of the process leading to being granted an interview.

RECOMMENDATIONS

Recommendations for medical school are usually letters written by people with whom you've had an academic or professional relationship during college. If your school has premedical advising, that office will often assist you with the process of getting your letters of recommendation. Professors and physicians whom you have worked with on medically related jobs are good people to ask for letters of recommendation. At some schools, a premedical committee will draft a letter of recommendation using the letters of recommendation from individuals you have chosen to recommend you.

When requesting a letter of recommendation, you should try to approach your potential recommender with all the material he or she will need to write your recommendation. This may include a copy of your resume, transcript, or any personal statement that you have written for your medical school application.

If you are returning to school after a few years out of college, you will probably need to handle the process on your own. You will still want to ask former professors for their recommendation, as medical schools will want to know about your academic readiness and intellectual ability.

Who you choose to write your recommendations is up to you. It's best always to approach people who know your character well and understand your reasons for wanting to attend medical school. There is no need to obtain more letters of recommendation than the schools you are applying to require. They will just add to the paperwork for the admissions committee and will not create a more favorable impression than letters from appropriate recommenders.

EXTRACURRICULAR ACTIVITIES

When trying to decide if this is the profession for you, nothing can replace good old-fashioned experience. Try to find opportunities to work in a hospital, clinic, or medical research facility. Along with giving you more familiarity with the field, your extracurricular activities will also serve as an indication to admissions committees that your interest in medicine is not just a passing fancy.

Admissions committees are always looking for more than just good grades and MCAT scores. They want to select candidates who are also caring and humane individuals. It's important to show that you are interested in pursuing a medical career for the right reasons.

THE APPLICATION ESSAY

Medical schools request application essays because they want to get beyond the facts and figures of your grades and MCAT and find out about you as a person. Think of your personal essay as an opportunity to let them know just why you want to be a doctor. A good essay will convey the relevant information about your experiences and goals. Take care to write, write, and rewrite your essay to avoid making any sloppy errors. You don't need to be a Pulitzer prize–winning writer to create a good essay, but a clear, focused essay is absolutely necessary.

MEDICAL SCHOOL TODAY

The field of medicine is so stimulating and demanding that it is no surprise that it attracts special individuals. Those who exhibit self-discipline and maturity, as well as a genuine desire to help others, are most likely to succeed in this profession.

Increasingly, the face of medicine more closely reflects the diversity of American culture. By the end of the twentieth century, about 42 percent of medical students are women, and more than 30 percent of enrolled students are minorities. Among minority groups, however, only the Asian population of medical students equals their proportion in the U.S. population. African Americans, Mexican Americans, mainland Puerto Ricans, and Native Americans are still underrepresented in medical schools. To bring the number of minority physicians into line with the general population, in 1991 the Association of American Medical Colleges launched "Project 3000 by 2000." This program was developed to recruit and enroll 3,000 underrepresented minority students by the year 2000. By 1994, Project 3000 was well on its way to achieving its goal, with 2,014 under-represented minority students entering medical school in the United States that year. In 1997, underrepresented minorities made up 10.6 percent of U.S. medical school graduates. Asian and Pacific Islanders constituted 15.9 percent of the graduating population, with other minority groups making up another 3.2 percent.

The Curriculum

Medical school for full-time students generally lasts four years. During the first two years, students receive instruction in the sciences that form the core of medicine: anatomy, biochemistry, physiology, microbiology, pathology, and pharmacology, as well as behavioral sciences. In most medical schools students also begin to acquire practice in patient interviewing and examination techniques. Whether or not patient contact is introduced in the first year or the second year, however, almost all medical schools introduce clinical problems early in the curriculum.

In the third year students are given more opportunities to gain experience with patients. This takes place in hospital, clinic, and office settings in the fields of internal medicine, family medicine, pediatrics, obstetrics and gynecology, surgery, and psychiatry. And finally, during the fourth and final year of medical school, you receive instruction through a combination of required and elective courses, along with more hands-on experience working with patients. The clinical clerkships of the third and fourth years allow medical students to develop their interpersonal doctor-patient skills and diagnostic abilities.

Toward the end of medical school you will choose an area of specialization and apply to residency programs. After graduating, medical students spend at least three years in a graduate medical education program, also known as a residency. This is also the time that you train to obtain your license to practice. Residency programs are discussed in the next chapter; subsequent chapters discuss the different specialties and subspecialties that make up the field of medicine.

CHAPTER 3

RESIDENCY TRAINING

Many people enter medical school already interested in practicing a particular kind of medicine. They may start their medical training secure in the knowledge that they will become a pediatrician, surgeon, or other specialist. During their training, they are exposed to the various branches of medicine, and while many pursue their original plans, others find they are drawn to a new specialty. In the final year of study, medical students decide what area of medicine they want to practice. After graduating and receiving the M.D. degree, the new physicians then enter a residency program to gain expertise in the specialty of their choice. There they gain the hands-on, practical experience that enables them to be certified by one of the twenty-four specialty boards.

A study in 1993 by the Association of American Medical Colleges (AAMC) found that 97 percent of students graduating from medical school planned to enter a residency program and become a certified specialist. While there were fewer than 600 hospitals providing residency training for

5,118 physicians in 1940, by 1994 there were 98,903 residency positions, distributed among 7, 228 programs.

The influx of women into the medical profession is reflected in the number of female residents. In 1988, 28 percent of all residents were women. By 1995, that number had risen to 34 percent. Women are most concentrated in internal medicine, obstetrics and gynecology, pediatrics, and family medicine.

RESIDENTS, INTERNS, AND FELLOWS

Residency is a period of training in a specific medical specialty. Medical organizations, such as the American Medical Association (AMA) and hospitals call this training graduate medical education (GME).

It is easy to be confused by the various terms used to describe the period of graduate medical education. In the past, medical school graduates usually spent their first graduate year in a hospital internship. For that reason, "intern" was used to describe individuals in their first year of hospital training. Many people still use this term when describing first-year residents in training; however, since 1975 the *Graduate Medical Education Directory* and the Accreditation Council for Graduate Medical Education (ACGME) have referred to them as "residents." The first year of graduate training after medical school is called the Post Graduate Year-1, or PGY-1.

Another confusing term is that of "fellowship." Fellowship is a term used by some hospitals and in some specialties to denote trainees in subspecialty GME programs. Again, however, fellows are more commonly referred to as residents. For the purpose of this text, the word "resident" will be used to describe anyone participating in graduate medical education, whether it is specialty or subspecialty training.

SPECIALIZATION

There are twenty-six approved medical specialties. They are governed by twenty-four approved medical specialty boards that grant certification. The following is a list of these specialties:

Allergy and Immunology
Anesthesiology
Colon and Rectal Surgery
Dermatology
Diagnostic Radiology
Emergency Medicine
Family Practice
Internal Medicine
Medical Genetics
Neurological Surgery
Neurology
Nuclear Medicine
Obstetrics and Gynecology
Ophthalmology

Orthopaedic Surgery
Otolaryngology
Pathology
Pediatrics
Physical Medicine and Rehabilitation
Plastic Surgery
Preventive Medicine
Psychiatry
Radiation Oncology
Surgery
Thoracic Surgery
Urology

Along with these specialties are subspecialties. A subspecialist is someone who has completed specialty training and gone on to take additional training in a more specific area of that specialty. For example, nephrology, which deals with the kidneys, is a subspecialty of internal medicine; child psychiatry is a subspecialty of psychiatry; and hand surgery is a subspecialty of general surgery. These specialties and subspecialties will be discussed in later chapters in greater detail.

CERTIFICATION

Certification is a process of testing and evaluation of physicians in a particular medical specialty. Every specialty has a different certifying board that regulates the practice of that area of medicine, and the length of required additional study after medical school varies from three to seven years, depending on the specialty. For example, specialties such as family medicine, pediatrics, and internal medicine generally require three years of graduate medical education beyond medical school. General surgery, on the other hand, requires five years of training; other surgical specialties may call for an even longer period of residency training.

Students who want to practice other specialties frequently enter residency programs that will provide them with broad clinical background. Thus, a future dermatologist, radiologist, or anesthesiologist may spend the first year working as a resident in internal medicine, entering their area of specialty in the following year. The determination of qualification is made by one of the twenty-four approved medical specialty boards that grant certification. Together, these boards form the American Board of Medical Specialties (ABMS).

LOCATION OF RESIDENCY PROGRAMS

Most residency programs are based in hospitals. Residency programs might also exist in ambulatory clinics, outpatient surgical centers, mental health clinics or agencies, public health agencies, blood banks, medical examiners' offices, or physicians' offices.

Geographically, residency programs tend to be in densely populated areas of the country. The residency program's goal is to expose the new physician to as many medical or surgical situations as possible. Rural settings have less variety than urban ones and don't give the resident, especially in certain specialties and subspecialties, as rich and diverse a clinical experience. New York has the most residency programs, and California ranks second.

HOURS WORKED

The number of hours a resident works depends on his or her specialty. The following table is drawn from physician workforce information gathered by FREIDA (Fellowship and Residency Electronic Interactive Data Access), which is the American Medical Association's electronic database containing information about each residency program. This table shows the average hours on duty per week of several specialties, as well as the average number of consecutive hours on duty for those specialties. These hours represent the average of those worked by *all* residents, not just first-year residents. In fact, first-year residents sometimes put in even longer weeks, working nonstop sometimes for two days at a time.

Specialty	Average hours on duty per week	Average maximum consecutive hours
Family practice	64.9	30.9
Cardiovascular disease	55.0	23.1
Endocrinology	43.2	17.5
Hematology	50.2	18.6
General surgery	80.1	31.7
Neurological surgery	75.9	32.3

FINANCING RESIDENCY TRAINING

The majority of medical students, about 81 percent, borrow at least a portion of the money for their medical education. In 1994, the average amount that medical students owed upon graduation was more than $63,000. That is a significant amount, but you should keep in mind that a medical education is an investment and the financial opportunities beyond graduation will enable you to repay educational debt.

The years of residency training, however, are not lucrative. In the late 1990s, residents usually earned salaries in the low to mid-thirties. Some residents supplement this income with money they earn from moonlighting. Of course, given the intense hours worked, you should not expect to be able to dedicate much time to extra work.

Benefits are also included in residency programs. Most residents get health insurance and liability insurance as part of their benefits package. Many residents also get meals and parking as a part of the benefits they receive. Less often, residents receive housing and child care as part of the benefits package.

NEW TRENDS IN GRADUATE MEDICAL EDUCATION

Just as the practice of medicine is changing rapidly, so is the training of residents. Medical practice is increasingly influenced by health maintenance organizations and managed care policies. Residents must learn not only how to recognize and treat diseases and injuries, but also how to manage a patient's treatments within insurers' preestablished guidelines.

The aging of America, the concerns about overly rigorous residency schedules, new regulations set by the government, and breakthroughs in understanding health and disease will continue to change the way physicians will learn to treat patients in the future.

Residents still work primarily in hospitals, but they are also spending more time with patients in outpatient settings. They work with more healthy patients than in the past.

Initiatives to limit the hours residents work will also change the nature of graduate medical education. Nevertheless, the years of residency will remain strenuous and exacting and will continue to be a most important part of medical training.

CHAPTER 4

FAMILY PRACTICE AND GENERAL INTERNAL MEDICINE

When we think of a family doctor, what usually comes to mind is the traditional general practitioner, or G.P. While the days of the housecall may be long gone, the medical specialty of family practice is still going strong. Physicians who practice internal medicine, another area of specialty that overlaps with family practice, also frequently fill the role of a patient's main, or primary care, physician. In this chapter we'll look at the philosophy and practice of these two specialties.

FAMILY PRACTICE

Background

After World War II, medical specialties began to expand rapidly. In 1940 three out of four physicians were general practitioners. By 1949 only two out of three were general practitioners.

Medicine was changing. Medical staffs were beginning to require board certification for physicians with hospital privileges. Residency programs in family practice were very limited, too. Even internal medicine was a specialty. So as the specialists gained status and popularity, the general practitioner was left behind.

When the general practitioners began to take steps to improve their diminishing status, they knew that one of their hallmarks was the interaction with patients and their families. So, the terms *family physician* and *family practice* began to emerge. By 1969, family practice was a board certified specialty. The next year, more than twelve thousand physicians were designated as specialists in family practice. By 1995, that number had risen to more than sixty thousand.

The Profession

The American Board of Family Practice (ABFP) defines family practice this way:

> Family practice is the medical specialty which is concerned with the total health care of the individual and the family. It is the specialty in breadth which integrates the biological, clinical, and behavioral sciences. The scope of family practice is not limited by age, sex, organ system, or disease entity.

The family practitioner cares for people from the time they are still in the womb through old age. The family physician is trained to provide comprehensive medical and surgical care, also called primary care, to entire families. If a problem is beyond the scope of a family physician, he or she will refer to another physician who specializes in the particular problem.

Even if a family physician does not treat a whole family, he or she always approaches medicine within the context of a family. In other words, a family practitioner always considers the patient as a social person, living within a family grouping of one sort or another. That means emphasis on the kinds of disease patterns found within a family, and paying attention to an individual's lifestyle.

Medical students are often attracted to family practice because of the diversity of the field. They can diagnose and treat and be around to see a patient's continuing progress.

Close and continuing relationships are also an attractive part of the family practice specialty. Most family physicians enjoy forming personal connections with their patients, whom they often know for decades. Family physicians thus are in a unique position to treat the "whole person," as they deal with their physical, emotional, and even social health.

Their wide range of skills also brings family physicians into direct competition for patients with other physicians. The specialties they most often overlap with are internal medicine, obstetrics and gynecology, and pediatrics.

Every specialty has its drawbacks, and family practice is no exception. Because of the nature of the care they provide, family physicians put in long hours. Because of their close relationships with patients, family practitioners are called a lot and sometimes have interrupted personal lives as a result.

Despite the long hours and hard work, family physicians make less money than other physicians. The average annual gross income for all physicians is approximately $199,000. The average gross income of a family physician is approximately $139,000.

All self-employed physicians must pay liability insurance. The average liability premium a year for all physicians in 1996 was $14,100; the average premium for family physicians was $8,400.

Training

In 1970 there were only 49 approved residency programs in family practice; by 1998 there were 489. The American Board of Family Practice requires successful completion of a three-year residency program. The only prerequisite for entry to a residency program in family practice is the completion of the M.D. degree.

Residents diagnose and treat both inpatients (patients who are staying in the hospital) and outpatients (patients who are not hospitalized). As they progress through their training, residents take increasing responsibility for all aspects of patients' care.

In addition, family practice training emphasizes preventive medicine, community medicine, and application of understanding of human behavior to the day-to-day practice of medicine. Family practice was the first specialty board requiring periodic recertification, using a written test at six-year intervals.

As the population of the United States lives longer, there is a greater need for family practice–based geriatric programs. This led in 1985 to the creation of an additional certificate program for physicians with an interest in geriatrics. Fellowship programs based in family practice residencies are also available—in geriatrics, obstetrics, sports medicine, and other clinical and educational areas.

In 1998 there were 10,501 residents in training in family practice. Over 44 percent were women.

INTERNAL MEDICINE

Background

The words "internal medicine" were used by German physicians late in the nineteenth century to describe a branch of medicine that did not use surgical methods of treatment with patients.

The American Congress on Internal Medicine was established in 1915 to facilitate exchange of ideas among physicians interested in this branch of medicine, to publish, and to grant research fellowships. This group became today's professional association, the American College of Physicians. In 1995, there were more than 115,000 internists in the United States.

The Profession

Specialists in internal medicine primarily treat adults, although some also treat adolescents. Internists, as they are often called, intimately understand all the major organ systems. They diagnose and treat acute and chronic diseases, usually from practices based in offices. They also visit patients hospitalized for problems that fall under the domain of internal medicine.

Every day internists see and treat a wide range of patients with an even greater array of illnesses. A typical day might see an internist treating colds and flus as well as diabetes, heart problems, and AIDS.

In medical school it is often said that internal medicine is an intellectual medical specialty because internists often diagnose and treat based on discussion with their patients rather than relying on extensive tests and procedures.

Some internists are board certified in internal medicine and another internal medicine specialty, such as cardiology or gastroenterology. This enables these physicians to have a general internal medicine practice, but also to be experts in a particular aspect of internal medicine.

Like family practice, internal medicine offers close and long-term relationships with patients. An internist is often in charge of overall patient management because of this relationship. If a patient has a problem that requires specialty treatment, the internist often coordinates that care. Internal medicine can be a challenging specialty because of the diversity and intellectual stimulation it offers.

As with family practitioners, internists must make themselves available to their patients. They may sacrifice more of their personal lives than physicians in other specialties.

Despite the long hours and degree of responsibility, internists are not among the highest paid physicians. Their average annual gross income is approximately $185,000. Their liability premiums tend to be lower than many other physicians, however. In 1996, internists paid an average of $8,900, just a little higher than family practitioners.

Training

Residency training for general internal medicine is three years. The prerequisite to training is the completion of the M.D. degree. In 1998 there were 21,714 residents being trained at 415 accredited residency programs in internal medicine. Of these, 37 percent were women. Board certification is granted through the American Board of Internal Medicine.

There has been a decrease over the last decade in the number of internal medicine residency positions filled by U.S. medical school graduates. The factors for this decrease are numerous. They include a decrease in the number of U.S. medical school graduates and an increase in the total number of residency positions in internal medicine.

Also, the newer reimbursement mechanisms for primary care physicians, such as internists, are not as good as they are in some other subspecialties. Reimbursement mechanisms are the rates at which insurance companies and the government reimburse doctors and patients for medical treatment and procedures. Interviewing patients and diagnosis, which are a large part of a primary care practice, are often not reimbursed at as high a rate as procedures that are more technological in nature. Therefore, this reimbursement system may be creating a financial disincentive for students to become primary care physicians, such as internists or family practitioners.

Because of problems in the past with overly long working hours and exceptionally strenuous workload, the Residency Review Committee in Internal Medicine established new residency program accreditation standards in 1989. New standards address such items as hours, which are stipulated as no more than 80 hours per week.

In 1998 residents in internal medicine spent an average of 66.4 hours on duty each week, with an average of 4.6 days off duty each month.

There are many subspecialties and certificates that are encompassed by internal medicine. The following chapter is an introduction to these subspecialties.

CHAPTER 5

MEDICAL SPECIALISTS

In 1970 there were 130,784 clinically active physicians who were identified as specialists. By the mid-1990s the number of specialists at work in the United States was well over 300,000 and rising. In all about 65 percent of the active physician workforce are specialists.

Internal medicine encompasses a number of subspecialties, which deal with different organ systems, a particular age group, or another area of expertise. As medicine has progressed, new subspecialties have been added to the list. One can expect that by the time you are ready to choose a specialty or subspecialty, the range of options will have again expanded, reflecting the dynamic nature of the medical profession. In the last ten years alone, for example, it has become possible for physicians to be certified in the specialties of nuclear medicine and medical genetics.

CARDIOVASCULAR MEDICINE

Cardiovascular diseases are the leading cause of death in the United States. Therefore, the subspecialist in cardiovascular medicine—the cardiologist or heart specialist—is in great demand for his or her expertise.

Cardiology is the subspecialty dedicated to diagnosing and treating diseases and malfunctions of the heart, lungs, and blood vessels. It is a highly challenging and intellectual discipline of medicine, combining diagnostic detective work with a thorough mastery of highly technological procedures.

As heart specialists, cardiologists treat a significant population of elderly people. And because of the significance of the heart in the human body, cardiologists are often right in the thick of things when patients have chronic illnesses and life-and-death emergencies.

Although in past years cardiology was primarily a diagnostic and medically oriented specialty, advances in the field have facilitated more invasive procedures. An example of this trend is cardiac catheterization, where a patient, under local anesthetic in an operating room, has dye injected into the arteries so that the cardiologist may locate any blockages. This type of complicated, invasive procedure has brought some cardiologists closer to being surgeons than they were before. As a result, cardiologists now divide themselves into two groups, invasive and noninvasive, depending upon how they practice the subspecialty. Common conditions that cardiologists treat include coronary artery disease, heart attacks, hypertension, life-threatening abnormal heart rhythms, and stroke.

In addition to diagnosis and high-tech intervention, cardiologists also place a high premium on prevention and are at the forefront of the preventive medicine frontier. Advances in knowledge about nutrition and exercise have helped reduce the number of deaths from heart disease.

Medical students who are interested in cardiology are often attracted by the challenge of this quickly evolving field. It is a subspecialty where diagnosis, high-tech progress, and prevention all meet. Cardiologists have a combination of long-term relationships with some patients and consultative roles with others.

Cardiology can be a stressful area of medicine because of the nature of its subject. Sometimes cardiologists deal with very sick people who cannot be helped. And because of the life-and-death aspects of their subspecialty, cardiologists often deal with problems that can't wait, which can interrupt the cardiologist's personal life.

There were 2,155 residents training in 199 accredited programs in cardiology in 1998. Of these, 14.8 percent were women. Training in cardiology includes three years of a general internal medicine residency with three additional years of training in cardiology.

Although there has been steady growth in the number of cardiologists, the increasing elderly population is likely to increase the demand for cardiologic services in the future. Most cardiologists have practices from which they treat patients.

In the past most cardiologists' practices were solo practices. There has been a shift recently toward group practices. About one-third of a cardiologist's time with patients is spent in hospital rounds. Many of their hospitalized patients are in special units called coronary care, or cardiac units. A small percentage are researchers only, and there are many opportunities for cardiologists in research. The average salary for a cardiologist is over $290,000, far higher than some other specialties.

ENDOCRINOLOGY AND METABOLISM

Endocrinologists diagnose and treat illnesses and disorders of the hormone-producing glandular and metabolic systems. Endocrinologists see a wide variety of diseases and have patients who range from very sick to those who need brief treatment. Endocrinologists are also often researchers, blending clinical medicine with research. In that endocrinology is unique, as few other specialties involve the same level of active research on the part of practitioners.

Endocrinology requires broad knowledge of other fields of medicine. Endocrinologists treat such disorders as thyroid conditions, diabetes, pituitary disorders, calcium disorders, sexual problems, nutritional disorders, and hypertension. Because of the nature of some of the diseases they treat, such as diabetes, there is a lot of opportunity for endocrinologists to use an educational component in their treatment, teaching patients with an ongoing condition how to manage their illnesses.

Endocrinologists work long hours. However, the analytical nature of the subspecialty is what attracts medical students and residents. And, although endocrinologists don't always know the outcomes of their patients' illnesses, their emphasis on analytic reasoning is a positive force in the field. Rapidly developing technology in endocrinology also challenges those pursuing it.

In 1998 there were 381 residents training at 130 accredited programs in endocrinology. Female residents made up 40.9 percent of this total. Three years of internal medicine are required with an additional two years in endocrinology and metabolism.

GASTROENTEROLOGY

Gastroenterologists diagnose and treat disorders of, or relating to, the digestive system. This includes the stomach, bowels, liver, gallbladder, and related organs. Gastroenterologists treat such diseases as cirrhosis of the liver, hepatitis, ulcers, cancer, jaundice, inflammatory bowel disease, and irritable bowel disease. Their caseloads are mostly made up of adults and the elderly, with infants and children forming only a very small percentage of their patient populations.

Gastroenterology is a procedures-oriented specialty. It requires a high degree of motor skill and manual dexterity. It also involves medical investigation, and gastroenterologists enjoy a good mix of patient care, diagnostic challenges, and procedures.

Some gastroenterologists say that a frustrating part of their field is dealing with patients who do not comply with treatments and with patients who wait so long for treatment that nothing can be done. It is also troubling to some that the procedures they must do are physically uncomfortable for their patients. These procedures include endoscopy, where the physician visualizes the hollow organs through lighted endoscopes. This allows the gastroenterologist to biopsy tissues and remove small growths.

Because of invasive procedures like endoscopy, gastroenterology is more surgical than it used to be. Gastroenterologists' level of responsibility is very high because of the invasiveness of some of the procedures they perform.

Gastroenterology is a lucrative field, although the hours are long, and there are emergency consultations on nights and weekends. The average salary of a certified gastroenterologist in 1996 was $223,300.

In 1998 there were 849 residents in 170 accredited training programs in gastroenterology. Of these, 15.4 percent were women. Gastroenterologists must finish three years of training in internal medicine and complete another two years in gastroenterology.

HEMATOLOGY

Hematology is the subspecialty that deals with blood and blood diseases, and with the spleen and lymph glands. Hematologists are researchers as well as clinicians. Many hematology training programs are connected to medical oncology programs, which probe the causes and treatment of cancer.

Hematologists treat all organ systems, but always related to the blood in those systems. They treat all age groups. This is a rapidly advancing field, and diagnosis and treatment often involve use of high-tech equipment.

Blood diseases are often serious or fatal, and physicians pursuing this field must be prepared for the stresses of dealing with critically ill patients. The rewarding aspect of this specialty comes with improving patients' lives. Hematologists treat leukemia, other cancers of the blood, lymphoma, sickle cell disease, hemophilia, serious anemia, and secondary problems that arise when a patient has another type of cancer. They also perform blood transfusions and biopsies on bone marrow.

Like many other subspecialties of internal medicine, hematology is very analytical and intellectually demanding. Physicians considering this subspecialty must be attracted and challenged by those rigors. And, because of the research and writing involved in hematology, it is a valuable asset if the person choosing this field is a good writer.

Hematologists must deal with the ongoing strain of death, even in the young, but not lose their compassion in the process. Because of the demanding nature of this subspecialty, personal time can be limited.

There were 205 residents working in 78 accredited training programs in hematology in 1998. Women made up 35.4 percent of hematology residents. Hematologists must finish three years of training in general internal medicine and complete another two years in a hematology training program.

INFECTIOUS DISEASES

Subspecialists in infectious disease diagnose and treat communicable disease. Traditionally, most infectious disease subspecialists worked at hospitals or medical centers where difficult cases would be referred. Today, however, there are more opportunities for private practice in this field. Infectious disease specialists are usually found in cities, where they can receive referrals from a large number of other physicians and thus practice their specialty.

This is an intellectually challenging field that requires some detective work. People are usually referred to these specialists when other physicians can't determine the cause of the problem. For instance, when a person has a fever that cannot be explained, the patient is often referred to an infectious disease specialist. The field of infectious diseases is very diverse, requiring the practitioner to have a wide range of clinical expertise.

This specialty has changed dramatically in recent years with the advent of AIDS. This aspect of the infectious disease specialist's practice can be very stressful because AIDS often strikes young people. Recent drug therapies, however, now allow some AIDS patients to live normal lives.

As with many other internal medicine subspecialties, infectious diseases does not involve a lot of procedures. For that reason, infectious disease specialists are not as well paid as some of the more procedures-oriented specialists. As infectious diseases are transmitted from person to person, usually through some form of contact, there is also a public health aspect to this subspecialty when outbreaks occur and affect whole populations of people. Most infectious disease specialists do not form long-lasting relationships with patients, with the notable exception of the case of AIDS, where the infectious disease specialist sometimes becomes the primary care physician.

There were 572 residents in training at 142 accredited training programs in infectious diseases in 1998, 36.4 percent of which were women. Three years of internal medicine residency are mandatory followed by at least two years of subspecialty training in infectious diseases.

MEDICAL ONCOLOGY

Medical oncology deals with tumors and cancers, which can occur in all organ systems. This subspecialty is closely

related to hematology. It is a multidisciplinary field because the medical oncologist treats all organ systems, and oncologists often consult with specialists in those systems. Oncology is a rapidly expanding and ever-changing discipline, and research opportunities in oncology are plentiful.

Oncologists who primarily treat patients must face the problems associated with close contact with seriously or terminally ill patients. There is a high patient mortality rate, and each person entering this field must find ways to handle the stress of dealing with death much more than most other physicians. It is important in oncology to have a support system of one's own to help with the emotional aspects.

Oncology, however, also provides lots of opportunities for getting to know patients well and having a high degree of involvement in their lives. Medical oncologists are often very involved with patients' families, too.

Because no two cases are alike, and because all organ systems are involved, the field of oncology is very diverse. Oncologists work on specific, practical problems and also examine larger, more theoretical issues. They are required to know a great deal about all aspects of medicine, and must depend upon referrals from other physicians.

There were 327 residents in 121 training programs in oncology in 1998. Women made up 25.1 percent of oncology residents. After a three-year residency in general internal medicine, an additional two years of subspecialty training in oncology are required.

NEPHROLOGY

Nephrology is the treatment of diseases and malfunctions of the kidneys and the urinary system. Nephrologists provide care for patients with kidney disorders, fluid and mineral imbalances, renal failure, and diabetes. They are involved with dialysis and consultation with surgeons about kidney transplantation.

Nephrologists see chronically ill patients, and they must have an excellent and broad-based knowledge of general internal medicine. However, like some other subspecialists in general internal medicine, they must also face the challenges of treating some very sick patients. Many nephrologists have patients who wait patiently for many years for a kidney to become available for transplantation.

Nephrologists, because they treat chronic diseases, get to know patients well and have lots of contact with patients' families. There is a high level of continuous care in this field.

Like many other subspecialties of internal medicine, nephrology is as diverse as it is intellectually challenging. Many facets of science and medicine are applied in nephrology: the basic sciences, chemistry, physics, and good people skills.

There were 635 residents in 135 accredited training programs in nephrology in 1998. Of these, 25.7 percent were women. Along with a three-year residency in general internal medicine, an additional two-year residency is required in nephrology.

PULMONARY MEDICINE

Pulmonary medicine is the treatment of disorders of the respiratory system. Pulmonary specialists, called pulmonologists, treat the lungs and other chest tissues. Pulmonologists treat cancer, pneumonia, occupational diseases, bronchitis, emphysema, asthma, and other lung disorders. They may test lung functions, probe into the bronchial airways, and manage mechanical breathing assistance. Pulmonologists often are found in critical care units of hospitals.

There is a lot of variety in pulmonary medicine, and pulmonologists consult with patients, perform procedures, and practice high-tech interventions. They see patients in outpatient practices as well as in the hospital. As in many of the subspecialties in internal medicine, the hours are very long. Because of the nature of their specialty, pulmonologists spend a lot of time in consultation with other physicians.

In 1998 there were 748 residents in 100 accredited programs in pulmonary medicine. Women made up 25.4 percent of pulmonary residents. After a three-year residency in general internal medicine, an additional two years of training in pulmonary medicine are required.

RHEUMATOLOGY

Rheumatologists diagnose and treat joint, muscle, and skeletal problems, including arthritis, muscle strains, athletic injuries, and back pain. They also deal with autoimmune diseases, such as lupus, which may have rheumatologic symptoms.

This is a rapidly evolving field. Rheumatologists are involved in prevention because some of the diseases they treat have been linked, at times, to lifestyle or nutritional problems. Because of the chronic nature of many of the diseases they treat, rheumatologists tend to have long-term, close relationships with their patients. Many rheumatologists say it is important to have good listening ability and compassion as many of the diseases they treat, such as rheumatoid arthritis, are very painful. Rheumatologists are, to a higher degree than some other subspecialties in internal medicine, extremely involved in the management of pain.

Rheumatologists can have more regular hours than many of their colleagues because there is little critical care involved. Many rheumatologists have office-based practices.

In 1998 there were 250 active residents in 107 accredited programs in rheumatology. Women made up 42.8 percent of rheumatology residents. Three years of residency in general internal medicine are required along with an additional two years of training in rheumatology.

OTHER SUBSPECIALTIES

Other areas of internal medicine include newer subspecialties. Fewer data are available about the newer subspecialties than exist for more established fields. Three of these new subspecialties are critical care medicine, geriatric medicine, and clinical and laboratory immunology.

Critical Care Medicine

Critical care medicine involves management of life-threatening, acute disorders—mostly in intensive care units. Critical care specialists take care of patients with shock, coma, heart failure, respiratory arrest, drug overdose, massive bleeding, diabetic acidosis, and kidney shutdown. Critical care is a subspecialty of these specialty boards: internal medicine, anesthesiology, neurological surgery, obstetrics and gynecology, and general surgery.

Geriatric Medicine

Although most subspecialties treat the elderly, geriatric medicine offers physicians the opportunity to intimately understand the needs of the elderly. As the baby boom generation ages, the percentage of Americans sixty-five and older will double, reaching seventy million by the year 2030. Only about 8,000 geriatricians were in practice at the end of the twentieth century, but it is predicted that the country will need as many as 36,000 in coming years.

The subspecialty of geriatric medicine is sponsored jointly by family practice and internal medicine. Practitioners must be familiar with the particular needs and treatments of an elderly client base, as well as understanding how to use resources such as nursing homes and social services to care for the elderly.

Clinical and Laboratory Immunology

Clinical and laboratory immunology is a subspecialty of allergy and immunology, pediatrics, and internal medicine. These suspecialists perform laboratory tests and complex procedures that are used to diagnose and treat diseases and conditions resulting from defective immune systems.

CHAPTER 6

SURGERY AND
SURGICAL SPECIALTIES

While the modern surgeon now uses an astonishing array of sophisticated techniques and tools, this was not always the case. The term "surgeon" was originally "chirurgeon," from the Greek word *cheir,* meaning hand, and *ergon,* meaning work. In the seventeenth century, surgeons were seen as socially inferior to other physicians. In fact, very few surgeons even had university degrees. While physicians were addressed as "doctor," surgeons were addressed as "mister." Barber surgeons used their razors to open veins for bloodletting, and to trim beards and cut hair.

Surgery has come a long way from the early days. Today, general surgeons and those in eight other surgical specialties are highly trained, very respected, well-paid members of the medical community. In this chapter, we will discuss these nine specialties.

GENERAL SURGERY

General surgery involves all types of surgical operations. Although general surgeons have heavy competition from the other surgical specialties, general surgery remains one of the most popular areas of specialization. It is often said in medical school that those who go into surgery seek clear-cut answers and results. They don't like the ambiguities and gray areas that arise in internal medicine, and enjoy the direct intervention of surgery.

A surgeon's hours can be long, irregular, and grueling. When a patient needs surgery, the surgeon must be there, day or night. Surgery is not a specialty that creates many long-term relationships between doctor and patient. Ideally, patients who need an operation improve after surgery, and no longer need the surgeon's expertise. Conditions that a surgeon typically treats are gallbladder disease, hernia, appendicitis, breast cancer, cancers of the digestive system, as well as emergencies.

The surgeon handles everything from minor health problems to profoundly serious diseases. Surgeons operate on patients of all ages, but because of the subspecialty of pediatric surgery, in some areas of the country, they treat mostly adults. There is a considerable amount of pressure in all surgical subspecialties because of the nature of the work and the responsibility that is placed upon surgeons.

Average gross annual income of general surgeons in the late 1990s was around $241,000 a year. Average annual gross income for all surgical specialties was around $275,000. Surgeons make excellent incomes, but many do have high expenses. Average annual liability premiums for surgeons were $21,700, for example. (That can be lower in some surgical specialties, but much higher in others.)

In 1998 there were 7,887 residents actively working in 266 accredited residency programs in general surgery. Women made up 20.5 percent of this total. A five-year residency in general surgery is required by the American Board of Surgery. Residents can begin their surgery training immediately upon graduating from medical school, without doing a residency in internal medicine first.

COLON AND RECTAL SURGERY

Colon and rectal surgeons deal with diseases of the intestinal tract, anus, and rectum. Until 1961 this specialty was called proctology because of the root *proctos,* the Greek word for anus. The name was changed to reflect the broader scope of the specialty.

Colon and rectal surgeons treat all age groups but primarily work with middle-aged and older patients. Although they are surgeons, these specialists provide a mix of medical and surgical procedures. An average day may involve some surgery, but also diagnostic techniques such as endoscopy, discussed in Chapter 5 under the section on gastroenterology. Colon and rectal surgeons treat hemorrhoids, fissures, polyps, cancer, colitis, and diverticulitis. Many of these diseases and conditions are easy to diagnose, and treatment has a high rate of success.

One of the most positive aspects of becoming a colon and rectal surgeon is the fact that you can diagnose and treat your patient's illnesses effectively. There is a lack of emergency situations, so colon and rectal surgeons control their hours more than in many other specialties. There is a good diversity of patients, ranging from the uncomfortable to the very sick.

Physicians in this specialty work out of their offices as well as in the hospital. A high degree of manual dexterity is required for this specialty, both because surgery is so exacting and for the diagnostic procedures used. Colon and rectal surgeons can give quick relief to patients who are suffering from painful conditions.

There are also opportunities for research in this field. Because they deal with colon and rectal cancer, new techniques for care and preventive measures are constantly being sought. Although their area of expertise is narrowly focused, the prerequisite training in general surgery gives these specialists a good, working knowledge of internal medicine. This is important since many conditions that colon and rectal specialists treat originate elsewhere in the body. The field of gastroenterology is especially related to this field.

Hours in this specialty are fairly regular, making it less demanding than many of the internal medicine subspecialties and some of the other surgical specialties.

There are a few training programs, and colon and rectal surgeons have one of the longest training programs in medicine. There were only 50 residents active at 30 accredited training programs in 1998; 20 percent of these residents were women. Completion of a five-year program in general surgery is a prerequisite to a one- or two-year residency in colon and rectal surgery. The field holds many opportunities for new physicians.

NEUROLOGICAL SURGERY

Neurological surgery, better known as neurosurgery, is the diagnosis, evaluation, and treatment of disorders of the central, peripheral, and autonomic nervous systems. Practitioners use high-tech equipment such as scan and Magnetic Resonance Imaging (MRI) to diagnose problems. They also meet with patients for regular physical examination in the office.

This can be a highly stressful and demanding specialty because it deals with the brain. The variation in outcomes is great; there are remarkable interventions and profound disappointments, as when a patient dies despite heroic intervention.

The brain is a fascinating organ, and we are just beginning to understand its mysteries. Many neurosurgeons say their work is less a career than a calling. They do it out of love of the subject.

The threat of malpractice is greater in neurosurgery than in some other specialties, and insurance premiums are extremely high as a result. The hours are long, and because neurosurgeons treat accidents and brain disorders that erupt suddenly, they may be called at any hour of the day. Yet, neurosurgery is challenging, creative, and constantly changing. And, because of the serious nature of the problems neurosurgeons deal with, practitioners get to know their patients well.

Neurosurgeons use their hands extensively, and a good deal of manual dexterity and technical skill is required. Neurosurgeons treat brain and spinal cord cancers, hydrocephalus, lumbar and cervical disc disease, aneurysms, and head and spinal cord trauma. Neurosurgeons must be excellent problem solvers, and they must also understand the logic of anatomy, physiology, and integration of the nervous system.

Neurosurgeons see a wide variety of conditions and serve a range of ages. They move between hospital visits, the operating room, and office settings.

Neurosurgeons rank among the highest paid specialists, often earning up to $400,000 a year. However, expenses, such as liability premiums, can be very high.

In 1998 there were 841 residents at 99 accredited training programs in neurosurgery. Of these residents, 9.8 percent were women. A year of a general surgery residency is required as well as a five-year residency in neurosurgery.

OPHTHALMOLOGY

Ophthalmology is one of several surgical specialties without the word surgeon in its title. Ophthalmology brings surgery, medicine, and diagnostic prowess to the diseases and abnormalities of the eye.

Ophthalmologists deal with sight loss, conjunctivitis, glaucoma, and cataracts. They treat the very young to the very old. Because they work on such a small and delicate part of the body—the eye—ophthalmologists must possess excellent eye-hand coordination and technical skill.

Ophthalmologists must be knowledgeable about optics, refraction, and visual physiology.

While some of their patients are only seen for one procedure, ophthalmologists have some long-term relationships, with patients who have vision problems, for example. Because they face few life-and-death situations, ophthalmologists deal very little with ethical issues, like the right to die or the rationing of medical care.

Ophthalmologists spend time in office treatment as well as in the operating room. They have some overlap with optometrists, who are not M.D.s and have their own schools of optometry not related to medical school.

Ophthalmologists' hours are much more controlled than in many other specialties. Annual average gross income is around $215,800.

There were 1,481 residents in 132 accredited training programs in ophthalmology in 1998. Of these, 28.6 percent were women. Ophthalmologists must have one year of general residency training, followed by at least three years of an ophthalmology residency.

ORTHOPAEDIC SURGEONS

According to the American Board of Orthopaedic Surgeons:

> Orthopaedic surgery is the medical specialty that includes the preservation, investigation, and restoration of the form and function of the extremities, spine, and associated structures by medical, surgical, and physical methods.

Orthopaedic surgeons, sometimes referred to as orthopods, often have broad-based practices, but may choose a narrower focus such as hand surgery, which is a subspecialty of orthopaedic surgery, or sports medicine, which is a subspecialty of family practice. It is often said that orthopaedic surgeons are mechanically inclined and like to put things together. The manual dexterity that they need serves not only in microsurgery, delicate spine surgery, and hip replacements, but also serves the practitioner well during casting and manipulation of fractures. Physical strength is also necessary for some procedures.

Conditions that orthopaedic surgeons commonly treat include arthritis, fractures, knee trauma, lower back pain, hip trauma, shoulder injuries, deformities, and degenerative diseases of the hip, knees, hand, feet, shoulders, and elbows. Because this specialty often deals with accident victims, there is a certain amount of time spent in assessing disability in legal actions.

One of the most positive aspects about being an orthopaedic surgeon is the ability to quickly relieve pain and to see patients leave satisfied and in good condition. There are lots of positive outcomes in orthopaedic surgery. Orthopaedic surgeons see a wide range of problems and a wide range of patients. It is as common to see children as it is to see the elderly.

Orthopaedic surgeons can work very long hours, sometimes twelve to fifteen hours a day. This detracts from a personal life. Their income level, however, is rather high. Annual gross income is around $341,000. But liability premiums are quite high, and the cost of office equipment, such as x-ray machines, is part of the overhead necessary.

In 1998 there were 2,771 residents in 157 accredited orthopaedic training programs. Women made up 6.9 percent of orthopaedic residents. Up to two years are required in a general surgery or other approved medical or surgical residency. Three years are required after that in an orthopaedic residency.

OTOLARYNGOLOGY

This specialty of surgery used to be called ENT—ear, nose, and throat, or otorhinolaryngology. In 1980 the name of the specialty was changed to otolaryngology—head and neck surgery. This specialty deals with surgery of everything above the shoulders. The exceptions are eye disorders, which are treated by ophthalmologists, and brain disorders, which are treated by neurologists and neurosurgeons.

Otolaryngologists see patients of all ages. Their specialty requires a range of skill because they treat a variety of problems both medically and surgically. Common conditions that otolaryngologists treat include hearing loss, tonsillitis, sinusitis, and head and neck cancers. Their surgical procedures are widely varied because they perform plastic surgery, delicate microsurgery, laser surgery, and major reconstructive procedures.

Otolaryngologists can be in competition with other specialties for patients. The specialties of thoracic surgery, plastic surgery, allergy and immunology, and pulmonary medicine particularly overlap with theirs. Some otolaryngologists solve this by becoming superspecialists, specializing only in facial plastic surgery, for instance, or otology (relating to disorders of the ear).

Otolaryngologists typically have fairly normal working hours and fewer emergencies than many other specialties experience. Annual average gross income is more than $300,000.

In 1998 there were 1,171 residents in 105 accredited training programs in otolaryngology. One or two years of general surgery are required before entering an otolaryngology training program, which takes three or four years to complete.

PLASTIC SURGERY

While plastic surgeons are perhaps best known for their cosmetic work on aging movie stars, most of their work takes place far outside the domain of vanity. Plastic surgeons help those born with deformities, or help burn victims regain a normal appearance. In addition to rhinoplasty for the nose and liposuction for the thighs, plastic surgeons treat a variety of clinical disorders such as cancer, congenital deformities, skin lesions, facial trauma, hand injuries, and degenerative diseases.

This is a highly creative field that requires a good aesthetic sense, attention to detail, and the ability to visualize and imagine. It is also a very innovative field with many new procedures on the horizon like artificial skin for burn patients and fat transfers.

Since plastic surgeons often improve people's appearance or lives, they can gain a great deal of satisfaction from having happy patients. One pitfall in this field can be patients' high or unrealistic expectations. Plastic surgeons see a wide variety of problems and a range of ages. While they sometimes have ongoing relationships with patients, most often they perform one or a few procedures on a patient and the relationship is over.

A high degree of manual dexterity is needed to be a plastic surgeon. The intellectual demands of the field usually come before the procedure; the plastic surgeon calculates the strategy ahead of time. Plastic surgeons require a combination of resourcefulness, artistic talent, and people skills.

Plastic surgery is very competitive. There are other specialists who perform some of the same procedures, like dermatologists who do skin grafts or otolaryngologists who do face lifts, and this intensifies the competition. There is a great variance in number of hours worked; plastic surgeons who are on-call in a busy emergency room may have long hours, while those who have private practices could have more controllable hours. Average annual gross income for plastic surgeons is more than $380,000.

In 1998 there were 466 residents in 98 accredited plastic surgery training programs, and 17 percent of the residents were women. The route to becoming a plastic surgeon offers options. Prerequisites are either a three-year residency in general surgery or a residency in otolaryngology or orthopaedics. A plastic surgery residency, after the prerequisite is satisfied, lasts at least two years. Many programs require physicians to do three years of plastic surgery if they have not completed residencies in any of the various prerequisite specialties.

THORACIC SURGERY

Thoracic surgery deals with surgery of the chest cavity— the heart, lungs, and esophagus. It is a highly specialized and demanding field and requires decisiveness and the ability to make life-and-death decisions. This specialty demands great manual dexterity and stamina. The hours are long, and the threat of malpractice is greater than in many other specialties.

Common conditions that thoracic surgeons treat are lung cancer, coronary artery disease, aneurysms, and heart disease. While patients of thoracic surgeons can be very ill, surgery can often result in immediate and sometimes dramatic improvement. Thoracic surgeons have a combination of long-term and short-term relationships with patients.

Thoracic surgeons' level of income is high. Average annual gross income is more than $325,000. However, annual liability premiums are also very high.

In 1998 there were 327 residents in 91 accredited training programs in thoracic surgery. Women made up only 5.5 percent of thoracic surgery residents. It requires the longest residency of any specialty. A five-year general surgery residency is followed by two or three years of a thoracic surgery residency.

UROLOGY

Although urology does not have the word surgeon attached to it, it is a surgical specialty. Urology deals with the medical and surgical treatment of disorders of the female urinary tract and the male urogenital tract. Urology relies heavily on diagnostic procedures, and medical intervention can be as significant in treatment as surgery. Common conditions that urologists treat include prostate conditions, malignancies in the genitourinary tract, urinary tract infections, and bladder disorders.

Urologists work with a range of disorders from the very serious to the uncomfortable. Many available interventions can dramatically improve a patient's condition. There are many newer treatments in urology including short, easier treatments for urinary incontinence, prostatic ultrasound, shock wave lithotripsy, and endoscopic surgery. Urologists need coordination and manual dexterity to perform their responsibilities well.

Urologists work primarily with adults and the elderly. They have a high number of long-term relationships with patients. Because they combine medical and surgical treatment, they divide their time between the office and the hospital. Urologists have long hours, but their income is very comfortable. Average annual gross salary is approximately $250,000.

In 1998 there were 1,080 residents in 121 accredited training programs in urology. Of these, 9.7 percent were women. A minimum of five years of residency is required. The first two years are usually in general surgery.

CHAPTER 7

OTHER SPECIALISTS

The previous chapters discussed general medical and surgical specialties. There are thirteen other specialties and many more subspecialties. Two of these specialties, pediatrics and obstetrics/gynecology, are primary care specialties. In primary care, patients and their physicians often form ongoing relationships. There are other specialties, however, that many people never have occasion to use.

Anesthesiology, an older specialty, is little understood by the general public. Although most people know that anesthesiologists are the doctors who put you to sleep before surgery, very few people understand the intricacies of the profession. Nuclear medicine, on the other hand, is a newer specialty that employs the exploding technology of the past few decades. An even newer specialty is medical genetics, which probes the genetic causes of illnesses, and seeks cures in genetic therapies. The other specialties covered in this chapter are allergy and immunology, dermatology, emergency medicine, pathology, physical medicine and rehabilitation, preventive medicine, psychiatry, and radiology.

PEDIATRICS

Pediatricians care for infants, children, and teens. Thanks to the advances in medicine over the past few decades, pediatricians see mostly healthy children, providing well-child care and guidance on prevention of illness.

Pediatrics is a specialty that calls for strong interpersonal skills, as pediatricians must deal with children and their parents. It is a very demanding branch of medicine and includes long hours and interruptions in the evenings.

Pediatric patients respond well to treatment and are often happy and satisfied customers. Children heal faster than adults, and this aspect of pediatrics can be very gratifying.

Although most of their work is with healthy children, pediatricians do see a variety of disorders. These include throat and respiratory infections, communicable diseases, cancer, congenital abnormalities, and developmental and behavioral problems. Pediatricians practice mostly in offices, sometimes in private practice, and sometimes in alternative settings like health maintenance organizations (HMOs). They also make hospital visits when they have very ill patients.

Like many of the specialties that are contact-intensive rather than procedures-intensive, pediatricians make less money than many of their colleagues. Average annual gross salary is around $125,000. Malpractice premiums are fairly low.

In 1998 there were 716 residents in 216 accredited programs in pediatrics. Pediatrics has always been a field that attracts women, and women accounted for 63.7 percent of all pediatric residents in 1998. A three-year residency in pediatrics is required. Subspecialization requires further training. Subspecialties of pediatrics include the following fields.

Pediatric Cardiology This subspecialty provides comprehensive care from fetal life to young adulthood to patients with cardiovascular disorders.

Pediatric Critical Care This subspecialist has special competence in advanced life support for children from the newborn to the young adult.

Pediatric Endocrinologist This subspecialist provides expert care to infants, children, and adolescents who have diseases that stem from the glands that secrete hormones.

Pediatric Hematologist-Oncologist This subspecialist deals with blood disorders and cancer in the infant, child, teen, and young adult.

Neonatal-Perinatal Medicine These subspecialists provide care for the sick newborn. They consult with obstetrical colleagues in planning care for infants of high-risk pregnancies, and they consult with pediatricians on the care of the very ill newborn.

Pediatric Nephrologist This subspecialist deals with the normal and abnormal development of the kidney and urinary tract from fetal life to young adulthood.

Pediatric Pulmonologist This subspecialist deals with the prevention and treatment of respiratory diseases affecting infants, children, and young adults.

OBSTETRICS AND GYNECOLOGY

Obstetrics and gynecology (OB/GYN) is a specialty devoted entirely to women. It entails two parts: gynecology, which treats diseases of the female reproductive system, and obstetrics, which deals with the care of women before, during, and after they give birth.

Obstetricians/gynecologists have some interesting issues facing them in today's medical environment. Biomedical research has produced profound advances in obstetrical care. These leaps have benefited patients, but have also led to higher, and perhaps unrealistic, expectations among patients. The threat of a malpractice suit following a delivery is of such concern that it has led some OB/GYNs to give up the obstetrics part of their practices and just practice gynecology. Others think that there is too much competition from other professional disciplines, notably family physicians and nurse midwives.

Another development is the relative maturity of women giving birth for the first time. This reflects the trends of the second half of the twentieth century as more women delayed having children until they were into their thirties. OB/GYN specialists must therefore be equipped to deal with new issues of fertility and childbirth that these patients present.

Most OB/GYN patients are healthy. If they are pregnant, their OB/GYN participates in a very important experience and time in their lives. But malpractice premiums, which can amount to more than $50,000 a year, are a major issue for this profession. This is also a specialty with erratic hours, and it makes many demands of its practicioners.

Conditions that an OB/GYN might treat other than prenatal care are yeast infections, pelvic pain, endometriosis, infertility, and cancer of the reproductive organs. OB/GYNs are medical doctors and surgeons and enjoy blending both of those aspects of their profession.

In 1982, 34 percent of medical school graduates planning to practice OB/GYN were women. By 1998, women made up 62.6 percent of the 4,881 residents training in 264 accredited programs in OB/GYN.

OB/GYNs are many women's primary care specialists and form long-term, close, and continuing relationships with their patients. A very small percentage of OB/GYNs include male infertility in their practices, but this is very unusual. This specialty treats women. Good manual dexterity is required because this is a hands-on specialty. OB/GYNs divide their time between the office and the hospital.

OB/GYNs have long, erratic hours and very high expenses, including liability premiums and office and equipment expenses. Average net income after expenses is around $231,000. In 1996, liability premiums for self-employed OB/GYNs was $35,200.

This speciality requires a four-year residency in obstetrics and gynecology. Subspecialization requires two or three years of further training. Subspecialties of OB/GYN include maternal-fetal medicine, which deals with high-risk patients; reproductive endocrinology, which deals with infertility; and gynecologic oncology, which deals with cancers of the reproductive system.

ANESTHESIOLOGY

The American Board of Anesthesiology defines anesthesia as a specialty that deals with the management of patients who are unconscious from causes other than surgery; management of pain relief and problems in cardiac and respiratory resuscitation; application of specific methods of inhalation therapy; and clinical management of various fluid, electrolyte, and metabolic disturbances.

In lay terms, the anesthesiologist manages pain and emotional stress during surgical, obstetrical, and some medical procedures and provides life support under the stress of anesthesia and surgery. Anesthesiologists must have a vast knowledge of physiology and pharmacology.

Many anesthesiologists can choose their own hours. However, there is a high level of pressure, because they face calls for quick decision making and life-and-death situations. If they are the only anesthesiologist on call at a busy hospital, they can have long hours in surgery. Anesthesiologists work with a range of health professionals and a range of personalities.

Anesthesiologists spend most of their time in hospitals. This is not a specialty that features close, continuing relationships with patients. Most of an anesthesiologist's contact with patients comes presurgically to evaluate the patient, describe the procedure, and help manage anxiety. Their last encounter with the patient is usually right after surgery.

The surgical procedures that they participate in range from the very routine, like tonsillectomies, to the very complicated, like open heart surgery. This makes their jobs very diverse. There is a reasonable amount of progressive technology in anesthesiology.

The unpredictability of the circumstances makes this a high-pressure field. Average net income after expenses is around $228,000, and liability premiums can be as high as $12,900.

In 1998 there were 3,708 residents in 147 accredited training programs for anesthesiologists. Women made up 26.6 percent of this population. A four-year residency is required for those who specialize in anesthesiology.

NUCLEAR MEDICINE

Nuclear medicine is a relatively young specialty. It is difficult to understand in some ways because it is so highly technological. Nuclear medicine grew out of the fields of radiology, internal medicine, and pathology. It is mainly a diagnostic discipline. For many years x-rays were the only way to see images inside a person's body. Today there is MRI (magnetic resonance imaging) and PET (positron emission tomography), to name a few procedures. These are the domain of nuclear physicians. They are approaches to diagnosis and are opening new vistas in the study of human disease. The word nuclear applied in this way refers to employing the nuclear properties of radioactive and stable nuclides in diagnosis, therapy, and research.

The Joint Commission on the Accreditation of Healthcare Organizations (JCAHO) has stipulated that all hospitals with three hundred beds or more should provide nuclear medicine services under the supervision of a qualified nuclear medicine specialist. These procedures are no longer the province only of academic teaching centers. Persons entering this field should be prepared for a rapidly evolving field and should thrive on problem solving.

High-tech equipment is at the core of the nuclear physician's specialty. Therefore, very few nuclear physicians are in private practice because the cost of such equipment is prohibitive. Most practice their specialties within the hospital setting. As a result, they are somewhat constrained by the hospital administration's willingness or ability to keep a department of nuclear medicine up-to-date.

It is often easier to secure a job after residency with the addition of training in radiology. Patient involvement is often limited, so those desiring long-term relationships with patients will not be satisfied with this field. Common conditions that nuclear physicians encounter include thyroid disease, cardiovascular disease, bone pain, and cancer. Most of their patient encounters are with adults and the elderly.

Specialists in this field have flexible hours and a high level of autonomy. Many enjoy the scientific precision with which they can diagnose an illness. Since they diagnose diseases from across the spectrum, there is a high degree of interaction with physicians from other specialties.

There were 128 residents in 76 accredited training programs in nuclear medicine in 1998. Women made up 27.3 percent of residents in nuclear medicine. A minimum of four years of residency training is necessary to qualify for specialty certification. Two years should be in an approved medical specialty, and two years must be in a nuclear medicine residency.

MEDICAL GENETICS

Medical genetics is a very new medical specialty, and it is one of the most rapidly advancing fields in medicine. Every physician who is trained in the twenty-first century will need to acquire at least a basic knowledge of the principles of medical genetics and will be instructed in their application to a wide array of clinical problems.

Medical genetics is both a basic biomedical science and a clinical specialty. Specialists in this field use their understanding of the genetic factors in health and disease to treat patients. Among the issues medical geneticists deal with are the nature of mutations, factors that affect development, and patterns of inherited characteristics. This field looks at genetic diseases and birth defects and probes into how genetic diseases can be managed. Medical geneticists are very involved in research, as this is such a revolutionary new field.

Disease prediction and prevention are at the heart of medical genetics. Because of the emotional aspect of predicting disease, physicians who want to practice in this specialty need to be very sensitive to their patients' emotions. Also, the novelty of this specialty calls for cutting-edge medical techniques and clinical practices.

Beginning in 1997, the Residency Review Committee for the American Council of Graduate Medical Education began accrediting clinical training programs in medical genetics. By 1998 there were 52 residents in 35 accredited training programs in medical genetics. Of these, 48.1 percent were women. A minimum of four years of residency training are necessary to qualify for specialty certification. Two years must be spent in a residency program in medical genetics. Because of the rapidly evolving nature of this specialty, the requirements for certification are certain to change over the coming years.

ALLERGY AND IMMUNOLOGY

Allergy and immunology deals with the human body's reaction to foreign substances. Allergy and immunology was officially designated a specialty in 1972 with the formation of the American Board of Allergy and Immunology. Specialists in this profession follow one of two distinct career paths: clinical practice or academic/research. This is a rapidly expanding field, with many opportunities for exciting research.

Those in clinical practice treat a range of ages from the very young to the very old. They often develop close, long-term relationships with their patients. The majority of their patients are generally healthy. Practitioners in this specialty have regular hours and a distinct lack of emergency cases.

Allergist/immunologists find that certain other specialties also perform some of their procedures. Depending upon which part of the specialty they practice, practitioners from rheumatology, hematology, otolaryngology, or pulmonology may overlap and create competition for allergist/immunologists.

This specialty sees many positive outcomes, and allergist/immunologists can help people suffering from allergic complaints feel much better and get back to leading normal lives. Often entire families have similar patterns of allergies. In this aspect allergist/immunologists are like family practitioners and sometimes treat the whole family. These practitioners spend some of their time with patients teaching them how to manage their allergies. Conditions that these specialists commonly treat are eczema, asthma, chronic cold symptoms, food and drug allergies, and AIDS.

Even for a physician only involved in clinical practice, this is a diverse field. Because it involves two related but separate disciplines, there is a latitude in the practice. Annual liability premiums are quite low.

In 1998 there were 205 residents in 79 accredited programs in allergy and immunology. Women accounted for 39.5 percent of residents in this speciality. Three years of residency in either internal medicine or pediatrics are required before a residency of at least two years in allergy and immunology.

DERMATOLOGY

Dermatology deals with disorders and diseases of the largest organ—the skin. Dermatologists deal with minor skin problems such as warts, acne, and eczema. But they also handle the removal and biopsy of skin tumors that demand expert diagnostic prowess, for dermatologists are called on regularly by other specialists to help figure out complicated diagnoses. Many dermatologists find they prefer either diagnosis or a procedure-oriented practice.

Other conditions that a dermatologist commonly treats are psoriasis, all skin cancers, sun damage, and contact dermatitis. Dermatology is a results-oriented profession, and dermatologists do have the benefit of seeing fairly quick results. They typically see relatively healthy patients. The noncritical nature of many dermatological problems allows for regular working hours.

Dermatologists spend most of their time in office settings. In order to diagnose well, dermatologists must be visually astute. Many diagnoses are made in dermatology on the basis of the way something looks.

Dermatologists have a mix of patient relationships, from short-term to long-term. Urban areas tend to be well saturated with dermatologists. Liability premiums are on the low side, but salaries are fairly high, averaging around $223,000.

In 1998 there were 853 residents in 101 accredited training programs in dermatology. Women accounted for 50.3 percent of these residents. The American Board of Dermatology requires four years of residency training including three years of training in dermatology. Subspecialization requires further training. Dermopathology, and dermatological immunology/diagnostic laboratory immunology are the two subspecialties of dermatology.

EMERGENCY MEDICINE

Emergency medicine is the medical specialty that deals with the immediate decision making and action necessary to prevent further disability or death. Specialists in emergency medicine are found primarily in hospital emergency departments. They are also responsible for setting up emergency medical systems in the hospitals. Because they don't have practices, most emergency room physicians aren't responsible for their own liability insurance; it is often paid for by the hospital. They have very little or no overhead because they don't have offices.

Emergency specialists treat all age groups. They make critical decisions on the spot about a patient's welfare, often without a medical history, sometimes when the patient is unconscious. They must be well versed in an infinite variety of illnesses and disorders.

Emergency specialists also must have good interpersonal skills and lots of composure. The hours are usually regular because emergency physicians rotate on a schedule. But most emergency rooms are staffed all night, and this means the emergency physicians often have shifts that are overnight. Switching back and forth from day to night hours can be tough. Holidays and weekends must be staffed in an emergency room as well. Although there is ample time off, shifts can cut into valued personal or family time. Nevertheless, emergency physicians' time off is usually completely free. When they are done with their shifts, they do not have to deal with work until they are there again.

This is not a specialty for those desiring long-term, close relationships with patients. Emergency physicians have no control over who their patients are; they must provide care to anyone who comes through the door. It is also important to note that some people use emergency rooms as primary care facilities. Therefore, emergency physicians see a good number of nonemergency situations such as flu, strep throat, and twisted ankles. But depending upon the location of their emergency rooms, these physicians also see major trauma like gunshot wounds and bad car accidents.

There were 3,239 residents in 119 accredited training programs in emergency medicine in 1998. Of these, 27.6 percent were women. An emergency medicine residency is three years long.

PATHOLOGY

The medical speciality of pathology deals with the causes, manifestations, and diagnoses of diseases. There are two main ways to practice pathology. One is in a hospital, investigating the effects of disease on the human body. These pathologists perform autopsies and examine tissues from patients. This is called anatomical pathology. The other way to practice pathology is as a clinical pathologist. These pathologists work in laboratories supervising testing procedures.

There are several issues of interest facing pathologists today. One is the effect they have felt from the tightening of the belt of government agencies and insurance companies. Most people don't pay for their medical costs entirely alone. But in today's medical environment, it is not as easy to have procedures and services paid for as it was in the past. Continuing efforts to cut costs in health care will affect pathology because most of the diagnostic tests fall into the pathologist's domain. Even a simple blood test is the province of the pathologist once it leaves the doctor's office where it was drawn. It's just that many patients never see the pathologists who help diagnose them.

Also of interest is the exploding technology in pathology. Now more than ever, pathologists can make significant contributions to medicine.

Pathology is a very scientific discipline, and there is little patient contact. There is, however, considerable contact with other specialists. Pathology is diverse, since it spans all medical specialties. Pathologists have regular hours. There can be more business management in pathology than in other specialties. This is because many pathologists have the job of running larger labs.

In 1998 there were 2,463 residents in 174 accredited programs in pathology. Women accounted for 42.8 percent of residents in this speciality. The American Board of Pathology offers certification either in anatomic or clinical pathology, or both. The combined certification takes five years to complete. Subspecialties of pathology include the following fields.

Blood Banking A physician specializing in blood banking is responsible for the maintenance of an adequate blood supply, blood donor and patient-recipient safety, and appropriate blood utilization. The blood-banking specialist directs the preparation and safe use of specially prepared blood components, including red blood cells, white blood cells, platelets, and plasma constituents.

Chemical Pathology These specialists deal with the biochemistry of the body as it applies to the cause and progress of disease. This specialty includes the application of biochemical data to the detection, confirmation, or monitoring of a disease. The chemical pathologist often serves as a consultant in the diagnosis and treatment of disease.

Dermopathology This specialty diagnoses and monitors diseases of the skin. The dermopathologist often serves as a clinical consultant and must have an in-depth knowledge of dermatology, microbiology, parasitology, new technology, and laboratory management.

Forensic Pathology A forensic pathologist investigates and evaluates cases of sudden, unexpected, suspicious, and violent death as well as other specific classes of death defined by law. This specialist sometimes serves the public by becoming a coroner or medical examiner.

Hematology/Pathology This subspecialist deals with diseases that affect the bone marrow, blood cells, blood clotting mechanisms, and lymph nodes. He or she functions as a consultant to all physicians.

Immunopathology This subspecialist is concerned with the scientific study of the causes, the diagnosis, and prognosis of disease using the application of immunological principles to the analysis of tissues, cells, and body fluids.

Medical Microbiology This subspecialist devotes expertise to the isolation and identification of microbial agents that cause infectious diseases. This subspecialist frequently serves as a consultant to primary care physicians when they are dealing with patients with infectious diseases.

Neuropathology Neuropathologists deal with the diagnoses of diseases of the nervous system and muscles; they often serve as consultants to neurologists and neurosurgeons.

PHYSICAL MEDICINE AND REHABILITATION

Physical medicine and rehabilitation (PM & R), also called physiatry, deals with diagnosing, evaluating, and treating patients with impairments and disabilities that involve musculoskeletal, neurologic, cardiovascular, and other body systems. The focus is on the restoration of physical, psychological, social, and vocational function and on alleviation of pain.

Physiatry is a broad field with many opportunities, both in practice and in research. Some physiatrists work in inpatient hospital settings helping to restore stroke or accident victims to a functioning life. This type of practice demands knowledge of, and intersects with, many interesting areas of medicine including orthopaedics, neurology, psychiatry, internal medicine, urology, and geriatrics. Other physiatrists have private practices and specialize further in areas like sports medicine.

A high degree of patient and family contact are typical in physiatry. The hours are regular. There is considerable opportunity for patient education, and there can be a great deal of satisfaction inherent in watching the progress that patients make. In addition to those conditions that already have been mentioned, physiatrists also treat arthritis, amputations, back and neck pain, and head and spinal cord trauma.

In 1998 there were 1,134 residents in 81 accredited training programs in physical medicine and rehabilitation. Women made up 34.7 percent of residents in this speciality. One year of a general internal medicine residency is usually required before a physical medicine and rehabilitation residency of three years can be entered, although some programs offer first-year residencies in this specialty.

PREVENTIVE MEDICINE

Preventive medicine encompasses general preventive medicine, public health, occupational medicine, and aerospace medicine. It requires knowledge and skill in management, epidemiology, health education and health policy, nutrition, biostatistics, and health services administration. Physicians in this field work in the armed forces, general and family practice, government, hospitals, and industry.

This is not a specialty that includes a lot of people contact. Using the preventive frame of reference, the community is the patient, and the physician's focus is on treating the causes of disease. These causes can include environmental factors, lifestyle, nutrition, or behavior. These specialists are in the public eye because they help make health policy decisions.

An interesting aspect of this specialty is that it often deals with people outside the health arena, such as politicians, lawyers, and economists. There is a community-wide or even global approach to this type of medicine, so the gains that are made have the potential to help thousands or even millions of people. Issues that preventive medicine specialists deal with include sexually transmitted diseases, obesity, cholesterol problems, teen pregnancy, environmental hazards, and smoking.

In 1998 there were 438 residents in 89 accredited training programs in general preventive health, occupational health, public health, and aerospace medicine. Women accounted for 33.8 percent of residents in preventive medicine. One year of clinical training is a prerequisite to entering residency in preventive medicine. Residency typically includes one academic year leading to a master's degree in public health, or equivalent degree, and one to two years of training in the field. Advanced training may focus on public health, general preventive medicine, occupational medicine, or aerospace medicine. Completion of a residency plus a fourth year of training is required in each of the subspecialties by the American Board of Preventive Medicine.

PSYCHIATRY

Psychiatrists diagnose and treat mental, emotional, and behavioral disorders. Although they have the same medical school training as other physicians, they often use some form of discussion as the basis for treatment. This can take the form of individual therapy or group therapy. Lately there have been great advances in the understanding of the biochemical effects of behavior. As a result, pharmacologic interventions are being used more and more often to treat emotional problems.

Psychiatry is most definitely a profession that calls for strong communication skills. Psychiatrists, more than any other practitioners of medicine, must use all their knowledge to understand the patient's point of reference. Psychiatry is much different than other forms of medicine because at its core it centers on a patient's beliefs, values, and goals.

Psychiatry is an intellectually rigorous and reflective profession. It demands that the practitioner challenge his or her own beliefs regularly. There can be a great deal of satisfaction in seeing patients gain confidence and improve their lives.

However, some patient's conditions are chronic, and the person considering psychiatry must learn to live with the fact that some patients will never get fully well. Some conditions like Alzheimer's and schizophrenia create long-term problems. Other conditions that psychiatrists treat include depression, anxiety, personality disorders, and chemical and alcohol dependency.

Psychiatrists who are self-employed can set their own hours. Gross annual average income is around $133,700. Liability premiums are quite low, averaging around $5,200.

In 1998 there were 4,595 residents in 192 accredited training programs in psychiatry. Of these, 45 percent were women. The American Board of Psychiatry and Neurology requires a broad-based first year of clinical training followed by a three-year residency in psychiatry. Additional training is required for the subspecialties, such as child psychiatry and geriatric psychiatry.

RADIOLOGY

Radiology deals with diagnosis and treatment of disease using radium-based substances and instruments. Radiologists formerly were trained in both diagnosis and treatment, but today separate programs exist for each of these aspects of practice.

Radiologists are primarily consultants. The diagnostic radiologists use x-rays and other forms of radiant energy to assist other physicians in diagnosing disease. Both types of radiology are mostly hospital based. Rapidly expanding technology demands that radiologists constantly update their knowledge to embrace an ever-expanding constellation of diagnostic and treatment techniques.

Although radiologists do have contact with patients, there is little long-term care involved in radiology. Conditions that radiologists commonly deal with are gastrointestinal complaints, cardiovascular disease, cancers, pulmonary disease, trauma, and hypertension. The hours are fairly regular, as radiologists are mostly behind the scenes in medicine. Average annual gross income is around $220,000.

In 1998 there were 3,831 residents in 201 accredited programs in diagnostic radiology, of which 27 percent were women; there were 450 residents in 82 accredited training programs in radiation oncology. A three-year residency in diagnostic radiology is required by the American Board of Radiology. The major subspecialties are nuclear radiology and pediatric radiology.

CHAPTER 8

MEDICINE IN THE TWENTY-FIRST CENTURY

Life is short, and the Art long; the occasion fleeting; experience fallacious, and judgment difficult. The physician must not only be prepared to do what is right himself, but also to make the patient, the attendants, and externals cooperate.

—Hippocrates

Never before has someone entering the medical profession had so many options. The field of medical practice has expanded beyond the wildest dreams of early practitioners. When a medical school graduate now takes the Hippocratic Oath, he or she enters into an occupation of many rewards and many challenges. One aspect of the medical profession, however, has remained the same: To be a good doctor, you must truly care about the well-being of your patients. The desire to excel at this profession must be based on the ability to focus, one by one, on the needs of the real people who come seeking your help and guidance in relieving their pain and suffering. This chapter touches on several of the issues and areas of interest in medicine at the beginning of the twenty-first century.

JOB OUTLOOK

Due to the expansion of the health care industries, which are expected to grow twice as quickly as the overall economy, employment of physicians will continue to rise during the first decade of this century. In 1970 there were approximately 240,000 physicians at work in the United States. By the end of the twentieth century, there were more than 560,000 physicians in active practice across the country. The majority of these physicians, seven out of ten, worked in office-based practices, including clinics and health maintenance organizations (HMOs). The rest were employed by hospitals and by the federal government.

Several organizations, including the National Academy of Sciences Institute of Medicine and the Pew Health Professions Commission, believe that there will be an oversupply of physicians in the years ahead, This is due in part to the increased efficiency and reduced costs demanded by managed care plans such as health maintenance organizations, as care for patients is shifted from physicians to other medical professionals, such as physician assistants and highly skilled nurses.

Although the prediction of oversupply of physicians is very real, particularly in some subspecialties such as gastroenterology, medical oncology, and hematology, the employment outlook for physicians will in general remain strong, particularly in rural and low income areas. These areas are what the U.S. Department of Health and Human Services call Health Professional Shortage Areas (HPSAs). More than forty-six million people live in such areas in the United States, 54 percent of them in inner cities, and 46 percent in rural areas. The need for highly skilled and motivated physicians in the HPSAs is critical, calling for as many as twelve thousand doctors in the coming years. For example, in these areas children are still dying of diseases such as measles, which should have been thoroughly eradicated by vaccination programs. People in the HPSAs also are more likely to suffer from high infant mortality, lead poisoning, tuberculosis, and AIDS.

The changing demographics of the United States has also created a need for physicians who are conversant in other languages and knowledgeable of other cultures. In some large cities, physicians now treat a patient population that speaks dozens of different languages.

Newly trained medical practitioners facing a shortage of opportunities will begin to serve these undersupplied areas, even though the salary opportunities are not as strong. On the other hand they will reap the rewards of practicing their medicine in an environment where they are greatly needed.

ALTERNATIVE MEDICINE

Currently, about two in five Americans say that they use alternative therapies when they are sick. By 1997 it appeared that Americans were more likely to visit an alternative medical practitioner than a primary care physician. The therapies that they seek range from homeopathy to nutritional supplements to acupuncture and meditation. Traditionally, the medical profession has dismissed alternative medicine as essentially voodoo medicine, rooted in superstition and mysticism.

Times have changed. Faced with the fact that many of their patients are employing alternative medical strategies, 75 of the nation's 127 medical schools, including prestigious institutions such as Harvard, Columbia, and Stanford, now include some training on alternative medicine. Medical students can now enroll in classes that introduce them to topics such as acupuncture, herbal medicine, and therapeutic massage.

This is not to say that alternative medicine has entered the realm of acceptance. Instead, there is a new emphasis on subjecting alternative medicine to the traditional rigors of medical research. In 1998 the alternative medicine office at the National Institutes of Health was transformed into the new National Center for Complementary and Alternative Medicine, with a budget of $50 million. This center will be involved in studying the effectiveness of alternative treatments.

PATIENTS' RIGHTS

Changes in the way that health care is delivered has changed the face of medicine. The role of health maintenance organizations and the increasing influence of insurance companies sometimes limits the ability of physicians to provide their patients with the care they believe is necessary. Physicians also must now spend more time on paperwork and record keeping. On the other hand, HMOs and increased insurance coverage allow more people to receive medical care, where they may have gone untreated previously.

Nevertheless, although medicine has never been more advanced, there is a sense of increased dissatisfaction with the health industries. The intricacies of HMOs and insurance policies often leave patients confused as to what tests and procedures are covered.

As a response to the growing concerns of patients, the American Medical Association (AMA) has proposed a Patients' Bill of Rights that would be passed by Congress and signed by the President of the United States. This bill of rights would require managed care plans to meet certain standards. The AMA has targeted eight key elements essential to patients' rights legislation. One of these is that decisions regarding "medical necessity" must be made "in a simple, timely process that is fair to the patient, the physician, and the plan." Another proposal is that patients should be allowed to choose their providers and must have access to specialty care where required. The AMA also wants the practice of health plan "gag clauses and gag practices" to be banned. These clauses and practices sometimes prohibit doctors from providing all the available information, tests, and procedures to patients who are covered by restrictive medical plans.

Insurance companies generally oppose such a measure, as they believe it will result in higher medical costs and thus limit the number of people who can be served. The debate over the cost and practice of medicine is likely to continue into the twenty-first century.

CONCLUSION

Modern medicine is undergoing revolutionary changes. Every day there are new discoveries, as physicians and researchers explore the outer limits of medical understanding. Where medicine was once the domain of the magic practitioner, medical professionals are now regarded as highly esteemed, scientific experts. They are also perceived as people who serve others, giving of themselves to benefit humankind as a whole. The influence of the medical professional, however, goes beyond simply curing diseases and repairing broken limbs. They also stand as teachers to the community at large, providing information to help people live healthier, happier lives.

MEDICAL SCHOOLS IN THE UNITED STATES AND CANADA

The medical schools and programs are listed alphabetically in order of state or province.

UNITED STATES

Alabama

University of Alabama
  School of Medicine
  Office of Medical Student Services/Admissions
  VH100
  Birmingham, AL 35294-0019
  205-934-2330

University of South Alabama
  College of Medicine
  Office of Admissions
  Room 2015, Medical Sciences Building
  Mobile, AL 36688-0002
  205-460-7176

Arizona

University of Arizona
    College of Medicine
    Admissions Office, Room 2209
    P.O. Box 245075
    Tucson, AZ 85724-5075
    602-626-6214

Arkansas

University of Arkansas
    College of Medicine
    Office of Student Admissions, Slot 551
    4301 West Markham Street
    Little Rock, AR 72205-7199
    501-686-5354

California

Drew/UCLA Joint Medical Program
    Drew University of Medicine and Science
    1621 East 120th Street
    Los Angeles, CA 90059
    213-563-4952

Loma Linda University
    School of Medicine
    Associate Dean for Admissions
    Loma Linda, CA 92350
    909-824-4467

Stanford University
    School of Medicine
    Office of Admissions
    851 Welch Road, Room 154
    Palo Alto, CA 94304-1677
    650-723-6861

University of California, Davis
    School of Medicine
    Admissions Office
    Davis, CA 95616
    530-752-2717

University of California, Irvine
  College of Medicine
  Office of Admissions
  P.O. Box 4089, Medical Sciences Building
  Irvine, CA 92717
  800-824-5388

University of California, Los Angeles
  School of Medicine
  Office of Student Affairs
  Division of Admissions
  Center for Health Sciences
  Los Angeles, CA 90095-1720
  310-825-6081

University of California, San Diego
  School of Medicine
  Office of Admissions, 0621
  Medical Teaching Facility
  9500 Gilman Drive
  La Jolla, CA 92093-0621
  619-534-3880

University of California, San Francisco
  School of Medicine, Admissions
  C-200, Box 0408
  San Francisco, CA 94143
  415-476-4044

University of Southern California
  School of Medicine
  Office of Admissions
  1975 Zonal Avenue
  Los Angeles, CA 90033
  213-342-2552

Colorado

University of Colorado
School of Medicine
Medical School Admissions
4200 East Ninth Avenue, C-297
Denver, CO 80262
303-315-7361

Connecticut

University of Connecticut
School of Medicine
Office of Admissions and Student Affairs
263 Farmington Avenue, Room AG-062
Farmington, CT 06030-1905
203-679-2152

Yale University
School of Medicine
Office of Admissions
367 Cedar Street
New Haven, CT 06510
860-785-2696

District of Columbia

George Washington University
School of Medicine and Health Science
Office of Admissions
2300 Eye Street NW, Room 615
Washington, DC 20037
202-994-3506

Georgetown University
School of Medicine
Office of Admissions
3900 Reservoir Road, NW
Washington, DC 20007
202-687-1154

Howard University
    College of Medicine
    Admissions Office
    520 W Street NW
    Washington, DC 20059
    202-806-6270

Florida

Florida State University
    Program in Medical Sciences
    Tallahassee, FL 32306-4051
    850-644-1855

University of Florida
    College of Medicine
    Chair, Medical Selection Committee
    J. Hillis Miller Health Center
    Gainesville, FL 32610
    904-392-4569

University of Miami
    School of Medicine
    Office of Admissions
    P.O. Box 016159
    Miami, FL 33101
    305-547-6791

University of South Florida
    College of Medicine
    Office of Admissions, Box 3
    12901 Bruce B. Downs Boulevard
    Tampa, FL 33612-4799
    813-974-2229

Georgia

Emory University
    School of Medicine
    Woodruff Health Sciences Center
    Administration Building
    Admissions, Room 303
    Atlanta, GA 30322-4510
    404-727-5660

Medical College of Georgia
  School of Medicine
  Associate Dean for Admissions
  Augusta, GA 30912-4760
  706-721-3186

Mercer University
  School of Medicine
  Office of Admissions and Student Affairs
  Macon, GA 31207
  912-752-2542

Morehouse School of Medicine
  Admissions and Student Affairs
  720 Westview Drive, SW
  Atlanta, GA 30310-1495
  404-752-1650

Hawaii

University of Hawaii
  John A. Burns School of Medicine
  Office of Admissions
  1960 East-West Road
  Honolulu, HI 96822
  808-956-8300

Illinois

Loyola University of Chicago
  Stritch School of Medicine
  Office of Admissions, Room 1752
  2160 South First Avenue
  Maywood, IL 60153
  708-216-3229

Northwestern University Medical School
  Associate Dean for Admissions
  303 East Chicago Avenue
  Chicago, IL 60611
  312-503-8206

Rush Medical College
Office of Admissions
524 Academic Facility
600 South Paulina Street
Chicago, IL 60612
312-942-6913

Southern Illinois University
School of Medicine
Office of Student and Alumni Affairs
P.O. Box 19230
Springfield, IL 62794-9230
217-524-0326

University of Chicago
Pritzker School of Medicine
Office of the Dean of Students
Billings Hospital, Room G-115A
924 East Fifty-Seventh Street, BLSC 104
Chicago, IL 60637
773-702-1939

Finch University of Health Sciences/Chicago Medical School
Office of Admissions
3333 Green Bay Road
North Chicago, IL 60064
847-578-3205

University of Illinois
College of Medicine
Office of Medical College Admissions
Room 165 CME M/C 783
808 South Wood Street
Chicago, IL 60612-7302
312-996-5635

Indiana

Indiana University
School of Medicine
Medical School Admissions Office

Fesler Hall 213
1120 South Drive
Indianapolis, IN 46202-5113
317-274-3772

Iowa

University of Iowa
College of Medicine
Director of Admissions
100 Medicine Administration Building
Iowa City, IA 52242-1101
319-335-8052

Kansas

University of Kansas
School of Medicine
Associate Dean for Admissions
3901 Rainbow Boulevard
Kansas City, KS 66160-7301
913-588-5245

Kentucky

University of Kentucky
College of Medicine
Admissions, Room MN-102, Office of Education
Chandler Medical Center
800 Rose Street
Lexington, KY 40536-0084
606-323-6161

University of Louisville
School of Medicine
Office of Admissions
Health Sciences Center
Louisville, KY 40292
502-852-5193

Louisiana

Louisiana State University-New Orleans
School of Medicine
Admissions Office
1901 Perdido Street, Box P3-4
New Orleans, LA 70112-1393
504-568-6262

Louisiana State University-Shreveport
School of Medicine
Office of Student Admissions
P.O. Box 33932
Shreveport, LA 71130-3932
318-675-5190

Tulane University
School of Medicine
Office of Admissions
1430 Tulane Avenue, SL67
New Orleans, LA 70112-2699
504-588-5187

Maryland

Johns Hopkins University
School of Medicine
Committee on Admission
720 Rutland Avenue
Baltimore, MD 21205-2196
410-955-3182

Uniformed Services University of the Health Sciences
F. Edward Hebert School of Medicine
Admissions Office, Room A-1041
4301 Jones Bridge Road
Bethesda, MD 20814-4799
800-772-1743

University of Maryland
  School of Medicine
  Committee on Admissions, Room I-005
  655 West Baltimore Street
  Baltimore, MD 21201
  410-706-7478

Massachusetts

Boston University
  School of Medicine
  Admissions Office L-124
  80 East Concord Street
  Boston, MA 02118
  617-638-4630

Harvard Medical School
  Office of Admissions
  25 Shattuck Street
  Boston, MA 02115-6092
  617-432-1550

Tufts University
  School of Medicine
  Committee on Admissions
  136 Harrison Avenue
  Boston, MA 02111
  617-636-6571

University of Massachusetts Medical School
  Associate Dean for Admissions
  55 Lake Avenue, North
  Worcester, MA 01655
  508-856-2323

Michigan

Michigan State University
  College of Human Medicine
  Office of Admissions
  A-239 Life Sciences
  East Lansing, MI 48824-1317
  517-353-9620

University of Michigan Medical School
   Admissions Office
   M4130 Medical Science I Building
   1301 Catherine Road
   Ann Arbor, MI 48109-0611
   734-764-6317

Wayne State University
   School of Medicine
   Director of Admissions
   540 East Canfield
   Detroit, MI 48201
   313-577-1466

Minnesota

Mayo Medical School
   Admissions Committee
   200 First Street, SW
   Rochester, MN 55905
   507-284-3671

University of Minnesota-Duluth
   School of Medicine
   Office of Admissions, Room 107
   10 University Drive
   Duluth, MN 55812
   218-726-8511

University of Minnesota-Minneapolis
   Medical School
   Office of Admissions and Student Affairs
   Box 293-UMHC
   420 Delaware Street, SE
   Minneapolis, MN 55455-0310
   612-624-1122

Mississippi

University of Mississippi
   School of Medicine
   Chair, Admissions Committee
   2500 North State Street

Jackson, MS 39216-4505
601-984-5010

Missouri

Saint Louis University
  School of Medicine
  Admissions Committee
  1402 South Grand Boulevard
  St. Louis, MO 63104
  314-577-8205

University of Missouri-Columbia
  School of Medicine
  Office of Admissions
  MA202 Medical Sciences Building
  One Hospital Drive
  Columbia, MO 65212
  314-882-2923

University of Missouri-Kansas City
  School of Medicine
  Council on Selection
  2411 Holmes
  Kansas City, MO 64108
  816-235-1870

Washington University
  School of Medicine
  Admissions Office
  660 South Euclid Avenue, #8107
  St. Louis, MO 63110
  314-362-6857

Nebraska

Creighton University
  School of Medicine
  Office of Admissions
  2500 California Plaza
  Omaha, NE 68178
  402-280-2798

University of Nebraska
  College of Medicine
  Office of the Dean-Admissions
  Wittson Hall, Room 5017
  600 South Forty-Second Street
  Omaha, NE 68198-6585
  402-559-6140

Nevada

University of Nevada
  School of Medicine
  Office of Admissions and Student Affairs
  Mail Stop 357
  Reno, NV 89557
  702-784-6063

New Hampshire

Dartmouth Medical School
  Office of Admissions
  7020 Remsen, Room 306
  Hanover, NH 03755-3833
  603-650-1505

New Jersey

University of Medicine and Dentistry of New Jersey
  New Jersey Medical School
  Director of Admissions
  185 South Orange Avenue
  Newark, NJ 07103
  973-972-4631

University of Medicine and Dentistry of New Jersey
  Robert Wood Johnson Medical School
  Office of Admissions
  675 Hoes Lane
  Piscataway, NJ 08854-5635
  908-235-4576

New Mexico

University of New Mexico
  School of Medicine
  Office of Admissions and Student Affairs
  Basic Medical Sciences Building, Room 107
  Albuquerque, NM 87131-5166
  505-272-4766

New York

Albany Medical College
  Office of Admissions, A-3
  47 New Scotland Avenue
  Albany, NY 12208
  518-262-5521

Albert Einstein College of Medicine
  Office of Admissions
  Jack and Pearl Resnick Campus
  1300 Morris Park Avenue
  Bronx, NY 10461
  718-430-2106

Columbia University
  College of Physicians and Surgeons
  Admissions Office, Room 1-416
  630 West 168th Street
  New York, NY 10032
  212-305-3595

Cornell University Medical College
  Office of Admissions
  445 East Sixty-Ninth Street
  New York, NY 10021
  212-746-1067

Mount Sinai School of Medicine
  Office for Admissions
  Annenberg Building, Room 5-04
  One Gustave L. Levy Place-Box 1002
  New York, NY 10029-6574
  212-241-6696

New York Medical College
　Office of Admissions
　Room 127, Sunshine Cottage
　Valhalla, NY 10595
　914-594-4507

New York University
　School of Medicine
　Office of Admissions
　P.O. Box 1924
　New York, NY 10016
　212-263-5290

State University of New York at Brooklyn
　College of Medicine
　Director of Admissions
　450 Clarkson Avenue–Box 60M
　Brooklyn, NY 11203
　718-270-2446

State University of New York at Buffalo
　School of Medicine and Biomedical Sciences
　Office of Medical Admissions
　40 Biomedical Education Building
　Buffalo, NY 14214-3013
　716-829-3465

State University of New York at Stony Brook
　School of Medicine
　Committee on Admissions
　Level 4, Room 147
　Stony Brook, NY 11794-8434
　516-444-2113

State University of New York at Syracuse
　College of Medicine
　Admissions Committee
　155 Elizabeth Blackwell Street
　Syracuse, NY 13210
　315-464-4570

University of Rochester
　School of Medicine and Dentistry

Director of Admissions
Medical Center Box 601
Rochester, NY 14642
716-275-4539

North Carolina

Duke University
School of Medicine
Committee on Admissions
P.O. Box 3710
Durham, NC 27710
919-684-2985

East Carolina University
School of Medicine
Associate Dean, Office of Admissions
Greenville, NC 27858-4354
919-816-2202

University of North Carolina at Chapel Hill
School of Medicine
Admissions Office
CB# 7000 MacNider Hall
Chapel Hill, NC 27599-7000
919-962-8331

Wake Forest University School of Medicine
Office of Medical School Admissions
Medical Center Boulevard
Winston-Salem, NC 27157-1090
910-716-4264

North Dakota

University of North Dakota
School of Medicine
Secretary, Committee on Admissions
501 North Columbia Road, Box 9037
Grand Forks, ND 58202-9037
710-777-4221

Ohio

Case Western Reserve University
  School of Medicine
  Associate Dean for Admissions and Student Affairs
  10900 Euclid Avenue
  Cleveland, OH 44106-4920
  216-368-3450

Medical College of Ohio
  Admissions Office
  P.O. Box 10008
  Toledo, OH 43699
  419-383-4229

Northeastern Ohio Universities
  College of Medicine
  Office of Admissions and Educational Research
  P.O. Box 95
  Rootstown, OH 44272-0095
  216-325-2511

Ohio State University
  The Ohio State University College of Medicine and Public Health
  Admissions Committee
  270-A Meiling Hall
  370 West Ninth Avenue
  Columbus, OH 43210-1238
  614-292-7137

University of Cincinnati
  College of Medicine
  Office of Student Affairs/Admissions
  P.O. Box 670552
  Cincinnati, OH 45267-0552
  513-558-7314

Wright State University
  School of Medicine
  Office of Student Affairs/Admissions
  P.O. Box 1751
  Dayton, OH 45401
  513-873-2934

Oklahoma

University of Oklahoma
  College of Medicine
  P.O. Box 26901
  Oklahoma City, OK 73190
  405-271-2331

Oregon

Oregon Health Sciences University
  School of Medicine
  Office of Education and Student Affairs, L102
  3181 S.W. Sam Jackson Park Road
  Portland, OR 97201
  503-494-2998

Pennsylvania

Hahnemann School of Medicine
  Admissions Office
  2900 Queen Lane Avenue
  Philadelphia, PA 19129
  215-991-8202

Jefferson Medical College of Thomas Jefferson University
  Associate Dean for Admissions
  1025 Walnut Street
  Philadelphia, PA 19107
  215-955-6983

Pennsylvania State University
  College of Medicine
  Office of Student Affairs
  P.O. Box 850
  Hershey, PA 17033
  717-531-8755

Temple University
  School of Medicine
  Admissions Office
  Suite 305, Student Faculty Center
  Broad and Ontario Streets
  Philadelphia, PA 19140
  215-707-3656

University of Pennsylvania
  School of Medicine
  Director of Admissions and Financial Aid
  Edward J. Stemmler Hall, Suite 100
  Philadelphia, PA 19104-6056
  215-898-8001

University of Pittsburgh
  School of Medicine
  Office of Admissions
  518 Scaife Hall
  Pittsburgh, PA 15261
  412-648-9891

Puerto Rico

Ponce School of Medicine
  Admissions Office
  P.O. Box 7004
  Ponce, PR 00732
  787-840-2511

Universidad Central del Caribe
  School of Medicine
  Office of Admissions
  Ramon Ruiz Arnau University Hospital
  Call Box 60-327
  Bayamon, PR 00960-6032
  787-740-1611, Ext. 210

University of Puerto Rico
  School of Medicine
  Central Admissions Office
  Medical Sciences Campus
  P.O. Box 365067
  San Juan, PR 00936-5067
  787-758-2525, Ext. 5213

Rhode Island

Brown University
    School of Medicine
    Office of Admissions and Financial Aid
    97 Waterman Street, Box G-A212
    Providence, RI 02912-9706
    401-863-2149

South Carolina

Medical University of South Carolina
    College of Medicine
    Office of Enrollment Services
    171 Ashley Avenue
    Charleston, SC 29425
    803-792-3283

University of South Carolina
    School of Medicine
    Associate Dean for Student Programs
    Columbia, SC 29208
    803-733-3325

South Dakota

University of South Dakota
    School of Medicine
    Office of Student Affairs, Room 105
    1400 West Twenty-Second Street
    Vermillion, SD 57105
    605-357-1422

Tennessee

East Tennessee State University
    James H. Quillen College of Medicine
    Assistant Dean for Admissions and Records
    P.O. Box 70580
    Johnson City, TN 37614-0580
    423-439-6221

Meharry Medical College
    School of Medicine
    Director, Admissions and Records
    1005 D. B. Todd Boulevard
    Nashville, TN 37208
    615-327-6223

University of Tennessee, Memphis
    College of Medicine
    Director of Admissions
    790 Madison Avenue
    Memphis, TN 38163-2166
    901-448-5559

Vanderbilt University
    School of Medicine
    Office of Admissions
    209 Light Hall
    Nashville, TN 37232-0685
    615-322-2145

Texas

Baylor College of Medicine
    Office of Admissions
    One Baylor Plaza
    Houston, TX 77030
    713-798-4842

Texas A & M University
    College of Medicine
    Associate Dean for Admissions and Student Affairs
    College Station, TX 77843-1114
    409-845-7743

Texas Tech University
    School of Medicine
    Health Sciences Center
    Office of Admissions
    Lubbock, TX 79430
    806-743-2297

University of Texas, Southwestern
  Southwestern Medical School
  Office of the Registrar
  5323 Harry Hines Boulevard
  Dallas, TX 75235-9096
  214-648-5617

University of Texas, Galveston
  Medical Branch at Galveston
  Office of Admissions
  G.210, Ashbel Smith Building
  Galveston, TX 77550-1317
  409-772-3517

University of Texas, Houston
  Medical School at Houston
  Office of Admissions-Room G-024
  P.O. Box 20708
  Houston, TX 77225
  713-500-5116

University of Texas, San Antonio
  Medical School at San Antonio
  Medical School Admissions/Registrar's Office
  7703 Floyd Curl Drive
  San Antonio, TX 78284-7701
  210-567-2665

Utah

University of Utah
  School of Medicine
  Director, Medical School Admissions
  50 North Medical Drive
  Salt Lake City, UT 84132
  801-581-7498

Vermont

University of Vermont
  College of Medicine
  Admissions Office
  C-225 Given Building
  Burlington, VT 05405
  802-656-2154

Virginia

Eastern Virginia Medical School
  Office of Admissions
  721 Fairfax Avenue
  Norfolk, VA 23507-2000
  757-446-5812

Virginia Commonwealth University
  Medical College of Virginia
  School of Medicine
  Medical School Admissions
  MCV Station, Box 980565
  Richmond, VA 23298-0565
  804-828-9629

University of Virginia
  School of Medicine
  Medical School Admissions Office
  Box 235
  Charlottesville, VA 22908
  804-924-5571

Washington

University of Washington
  School of Medicine
  Admissions Office
  Health Sciences Center A-300, Box 356340
  Seattle, WA 98195
  206-543-7212

West Virginia

Marshall University
  School of Medicine
  Admissions Office
  1542 Spring Valley Drive
  Huntington, WV 25704
  304-696-7312

West Virginia University
  School of Medicine
  Office of Admissions and Records
  Health Sciences Center
  P.O. Box 9815
  Morgantown, WV 26506
  304-293-3521

Wisconsin

Medical College of Wisconsin
  Office of Admissions and Registrar
  8701 Watertown Plank Road
  Milwaukee, WI 53226
  414-456-8246

University of Wisconsin Medical School
  Admissions Committee
  Medical Sciences Center, Room 1250
  1300 University Avenue
  Madison, WI 53706
  608-263-4925

CANADA

Alberta

University of Alberta
  Faculty of Medicine and Oral Health Sciences
  Admissions Officer
  2-45 Medical Sciences Building
  Edmonton, Alberta
  Canada T6G 2H7
  403-492-6350

University of Calgary
 Faculty of Medicine
 Office of Admissions
 3330 Hospital Drive, NW
 Calgary, Alberta
 Canada T2N 4N1
 403-220-6849

British Columbia

University of British Columbia
 Faculty of Medicine
 Office of the Dean, Admissions Office
 317-2194 Health Sciences Mall
 Vancouver, British Columbia
 Canada V6T 1Z3
 604-822-4482

Manitoba

University of Manitoba
 Faculty of Medicine
 Chair, Admissions Committee
 753 McDermot Avenue
 Winnipeg, Manitoba
 Canada R3E 0W3
 204-789-3569

Newfoundland

Memorial University of Newfoundland
 Faculty of Medicine
 Chair, Committee on Admissions
 St. John's, Newfoundland
 Canada A1B 3V6
 709-737-6615

Nova Scotia

Dalhousie University
 Faculty of Medicine
 Admissions Coordinator
 Room C-23, Lower Level
 Clinical Research Centre
 5849 University Avenue

Halifax, Nova Scotia
Canada B3H 4H7
902-494-1874

Ontario

McMaster University
  School of Medicine
  Admissions and Records
  HSC Room 1B7–Health Sciences Center
  1200 Main Street West
  Hamilton, Ontario
  Canada L8N 3Z5
  905-525-9140, Ext. 22114

Queen's University
  Faculty of Medicine
  Admissions Office
  Kingston, Ontario
  Canada K7L 3N6
  613-545-2542

University of Ottawa
  Faculty of Medicine
  Admissions, 451 Smyth Road
  Ottawa, Ontario
  Canada K1H 8M5
  613-562-5409

University of Toronto
  Faculty of Medicine
  Attention: Admissions Office
  Toronto, Ontario
  Canada M5S 1A8
  416-978-2717

University of Western Ontario
  Faculty of Medicine and Dentistry
  Health Sciences Addition
  Admissions Office
  Health Sciences Center, Room H-104
  London, Ontario
  Canada N6A 5C1
  519-661-3744

Quebec

McGill University
  Faculty of Medicine
  Admissions Office
  3655 Drummond Street
  Montreal, Quebec
  Canada H3G 1Y6
  514-398-3517

Université Laval
  Faculty of Medicine
  Secretary, Admission Committee
  Ste-Foy, Quebec
  Canada G1K 7P4
  418-656-2131, Ext. 2492

University of Montreal
  Faculty of Medicine
  Committee on Admission
  P.O. Box 6128, Station Centre-Ville
  Montreal, Quebec
  Canada H3C 3J7
  514-343-6265

University of Sherbrooke
  Faculty of Medicine
  Admission Office
  Sherbrooke, Quebec
  Canada J1H 5N4
  819-564-5208

Saskatchewan

University of Saskatchewan
  College of Medicine
  Secretary, Admissions
  B103 Health Sciences Building
  Saskatoon, Saskatchewan
  Canada S7N 0W0
  306-966-8554

COMBINED DEGREE PROGRAMS

The following is a list of medical schools that, in collaboration with their undergraduate division, accept high school seniors or undergraduates who have completed one or two years of study. In some cases, study towards the M.D. may be completed in less than eight years.

The list is organized alphabetically by state, providing the school name, address, and phone number. E-mail addresses are included, if available.

Alabama

University of Alabama School of Medicine—Early Medical School
    Admission Program
  UAB Office of Enrollment Management
  272 Hill University Center
  Birmingham, AL 35294
  205-934-8152

University of South Alabama
  Office of Admissions
  Administrative Building, Room 182
  Mobile, AL 36688-0002
  205-460-6141 or 800-872-5247

California

University of Southern California
  College of Letters, Arts and Sciences
  University of Southern California
  CAS 100, University Park
  Los Angeles, CA 90089-0152
  213-740-5930
  cas@mizar.usc.edu

District of Columbia

George Washington University School of Medicine and Columbian College
  Office of Admissions
  George Washington University
  2121 "I" Street NW
  Washington, DC 20052
  800-447-3765

Howard University
  Dr. G. Aboko-Cole, Director
  Center for Preprofessional Education
  P.O. Box 473
  Administration Building
  Washington, DC 20059
  202-806-7231

Florida

University of Miami—Medical Scholars Program Information
  Office of Admissions
  P.O. Box 248025
  Coral Gables, FL 33124
  305-284-4323
  (state residents only)

Illinois

Northwestern University—Honors Program in Medical Education
  Office of Admission and Financial Aid
  1801 Hinman Avenue
  Evanston, IL 60204-3060
  708-491-7271
  ug-admission@nwu.edu

Louisiana

Louisiana State University-School of Medicine in New Orleans
Office of Student Admissions
1901 Perdido Street
New Orleans, LA 70112-1393
504-568-6262
(state residents only)

Louisiana State University-School of Medicine in Shreveport
Office of Student Admissions
P.O. Box 33932
Shreveport, LA 71130-3932
318-675-5190
(state residents only)

Massachusetts

Boston University
Associate Director, Admissions
121 Bay State Road
Boston, MA 02215
617-353-2330
admissions@bu.edu

Michigan

Michigan State University—Advanced Baccalaureate
Learning Experience
College of Human Medicine
Office of Admissions
A-239 Life Sciences
East Lansing, MI 48824
517-353-9620

University of Michigan
Interflex Program
5113 Medical Science I Building, Wing C
Ann Arbor, MI 48109-0611
313-764-9534

Missouri

University of Missouri—Kansas City 6-Year Program
    School of Medicine
    Council on Selection
    2411 Holmes
    Kansas City, MO 64108
    816-235-1870

New York

New York University—Prehealth Office
    Admissions Office
    College of Arts & Science
    22 Washington Square North
    Room 904 Main Building
    New York, NY 10003
    212-998-4500
    prehealth@nyu.edu

University of Rochester
    Program Coordinator
    Rochester Early Medical Scholars
    Meliora Hall
    Rochester, NY 14627
    716-275-3221

Ohio

Case Western Reserve University—Pre-professional Scholars Program
        in Medicine
    Office of Undergraduate Admission
    10900 Euclid Avenue
    Cleveland, OH 44106-7055
    216-368-4450
    xx329@po.cwru.edu

Rhode Island

Brown University
    Program in Liberal Medical Education Office
    Box G—A134
    Providence, RI 02912
    401-863-2450

Tennessee

East Tennessee State University
  Director, Premedical—Medical Program
  Office of Medical Professions Advisement
  P.O. Box 70,592
  Johnson City, TN 37614-0592
  615-929-5602

Wisconsin

University of Wisconsin—Madison Medical School
  Medical Scholars Program
  1300 University Avenue, Room 1250
  Madison, WI 53706
  608-263-7561
  (state residents only)

The following medical schools accept high school seniors or undergraduates in collaboration with the undergraduate divisions of affiliated institutions. The list is organized alphabetically by state and gives both the medical school (MD) as well as the affiliated undergraduate institution or institutions (UG).

California

University of California, Los Angeles School of Medicine (MD)

University of California, Riverside (UG)
  Student Affairs Officer
  Division of Biomedical Sciences
  University of California, Riverside
  Riverside, CA 92521-0121
  909-787-4333

Illinois

Chicago Medical School (MD)

Illinois Institute of Technology (UG)
    Director of Admissions
    B.S./M.D. Program
    Illinois Institute of Technology
    10 West Thirty-Third Street
    Chicago, IL 60616
    312-567-3025
    outside of Chicago, 800-448-2329

New Jersey

UMDNJ—New Jersey Medical School (MD)

Boston University, Drew University, Montclair State University,
        New Jersey Institute of Technology, Stevens Institute of
        Technology, Richard Stockton College of New Jersey,
        The College of New Jersey (UG)
    Office of Admissions
    New Jersey Medical School
    C-653 MSB
    185 South Orange Avenue
    Newark, NJ 07103-2714
    201-982-4631

UMDNJ—Robert Wood Johnson Medical School (MD)

Rutgers University (UG)
    Bachelor/Medical Degree Program
    Nelson Biological Laboratory
    Rutgers University
    P.O. Box 1059
    Piscataway, NJ 08855-1059
    908-445-5270

New York

Albany Medical College (MD)

Rensselaer Polytechnic Institute (UG)—Accelerated
        Biomedical Program

Admissions Counselor
Rensselaer Polytechnic Institute
Troy, NY 12180
518-276-6216

Albany Medical College (MD)

Siena College (UG)
Office of Admissions
Siena College
Route 9
Loudonville, NY 12211
518-783-2423

Albany Medical College (MD)

Union College (UG)—Seven-Year Medical Education Program
Associate Dean of Admissions
Union College
Schenectady, NY 12308
518-388-6112

City University of New York Medical School (MD)

Sophie Davis School of Biomedical Education (UG)
Office of Admissions
Sophie Davis School of Biomedical Education
Y Building, Room 705N
138th Street & Convent Avenue
New York, NY 10031
212-650-7707 or 7712
(state residents only)

SUNY—Brooklyn College of Medicine (MD)

Brooklyn College (UG)
Director of Admissions
Brooklyn College
1602 James Hall
Brooklyn, NY 11210
718-951-5044

SUNY—Syracuse (MD)

Binghamton University (UG)
    Rural Primary Care Recruitment Programs
    College of Medicine
    State University of New York
    Health Science Center at Syracuse
    P.O. Box 1000
    Binghamton, NY 13902
    607-770-8618
    davismatt@hscsyr.edu

Ohio

Northeastern Ohio Universities College of Medicine (MD)

Kent State University, University of Akron, Youngstown
        State University (UG)
    Associate Director of Admissions
    Northeastern Ohio Universities College of Medicine
    4209 State Route 44
    P.O. Box 95
    Rootstown, OH 44272-0095
    216-325-2511
    admission@neoucom.edu

Pennsylvania

Jefferson Medical College (MD)—Penn State Accelerated Program

Pennsylvania State University (UG)
    Undergraduate Admissions
    Pennsylvania State University
    201 Shields Building—Box 3000
    University Park, PA 16802
    814-865-5471

Allegheny University of the Health Sciences (formerly MCP Hahnemann
        School of Medicine) (MD)

Lehigh University (UG)
    Office of Admissions
    27 Memorial Drive West
    Bethlehem, PA 18105
    610-758-3100

Allegheny University of the Health Sciences

(formerly MCP Hahnemann School of Medicine) (MD)

Villanova University (UG)
  Office of Undergraduate Admissions
  Villanova University
  800 Lancaster Avenue
  Villanova, PA 19085-1699
  800-338-7927

Tennessee

Meharry Medical College (MD)

Fisk University (UG)
  Henry A. Moses, Ph.D.
  Associate Vice President for College Relations and Lifelong Learning
  1005 D. B. Todd, Jr. Boulevard
  Nashville, TN 37208
  615-327-6425

Texas

Baylor College of Medicine (MD)

Rice University (UG)
  Office of Admissions
  One Baylor Plaza
  Room 106A
  Houston, TX 77030
  713-798-4841

Virginia

Eastern Virginia Medical School (MD)

The College of William and Mary, Old Dominion University, Hampton
    University, Norfolk State University (UG)
  Office of Admissions
  Eastern Virginia Medical School
  721 Fairfax Avenue
  Norfolk, VA 23507-2000
  804-446-5812

The Association of American Medical Colleges publication, *Medical School Admissions Requirements (MSAR),* provides detailed descriptions of the programs that combine the baccalaureate degree with an M.D. degree.

SPECIALTY BOARDS

Allergy and Immunology

American Board of Allergy and Immunology
  University City Science Center
  3624 Market Street
  Philadelphia, PA 19104-2675

Anesthesiology

American Board of Anesthesiology
  4101 Lake Boone Trail
  Raleigh, NC 27607-7506

Colon and Rectal Surgery

American Board of Colon and Rectal Surgery
  20600 Eureka Road, Suite 713
  Taylor, MI 48180

Dermatology

American Board of Dermatology
  Henry Ford Hospital, One Ford Plaza
  Detroit, MI 48202

Emergency Medicine

American Board of Emergency Medicine
  3000 Coolidge Road
  East Lansing, MI 48823-6319

Family Practice

American Board of Family Practice
   2228 Young Drive
   Lexington, KY 40505

Internal Medicine

American Board of Internal Medicine
   University City Science Center
   3624 Market Street
   Philadelphia, PA 19104-2675

Medical Genetics

American Board of Medical Genetics
   9650 Rockville Pike
   Bethesda, MD 20814-3998

Neurological Surgery

American Board of Neurological Surgery
   6550 Fannin Street, Suite 2139
   Houston, TX 77030-2701

Nuclear Medicine

American Board of Nuclear Medicine
   900 Veteran Avenue
   Los Angeles, CA 90024-1786

Obstetrics & Gynecology

American Board of Obstetrics and Gynecology
   2915 Vine Street, Suite 300
   Dallas, TX 75204-1069

Ophthalmology

American Board of Ophthalmology
   111 Presidential Boulevard, Suite 241
   Bala Cynwyd, PA 19004

Orthopaedic Surgery

American Board of Orthopaedic Surgery
    400 Silver Cedar Court
    Chapel Hill, NC 27514

Otolaryngology

American Board of Otolaryngology
    2211 Norfolk, Suite 800
    Houston, TX 77098-4044

Pathology

American Board of Pathology
    P.O. Box 25915
    Tampa, FL 33622-5915

Pediatrics

American Board of Pediatrics
    111 Silver Cedar Court
    Chapel Hill, NC 27514-1651

Physical Medicine and Rehabilitation

American Board of Physical Medicine and Rehabilitation
    Norwest Center, Suite 674
    21 First Street, SW
    Rochester, MN 55902-3009

Plastic Surgery

American Board of Plastic Surgery
    Seven Penn Center, Suite 400
    1635 Market Street
    Philadelphia, PA 19103-2204

Preventive Medicine

American Board of Preventive Medicine
    9950 West Lawrence Avenue, Suite 106
    Schiller Park, IL 60176

Psychiatry and Neurology

American Board of Psychiatry and Neurology
  500 Lake Cook Road, #335
  Deerfield, IL 60015

Radiology

American Board of Radiology
  5255 East Williams Circle, Suite 6800
  Tucson, AZ 85711

Surgery

American Board of Surgery
  1617 John F. Kennedy Boulevard, Suite 860
  Philadelphia, PA 19103-1847

Thoracic Surgery

American Board of Thoracic Surgery
  One Rotary Center, Suite 803
  Evanston, IL 60201

Urology

American Board of Urology
  31700 Telegraph Road, Suite 150
  Binghams Farms, MI 48025

ACADEMIC AND PROFESSIONAL ASSOCIATIONS

The Association of American Medical Colleges (AAMC) maintains a list of the academic and professional associations representing more than seventy-five thousand medical faculty members. Following is a list of the American Council of Academic Societies (CAS) member organizations, listed by discipline. These societies are intimately involved with research, training, certification, and public policy advocacy in the medical profession. Detailed information, addresses, e-mail addresses, and web links can be found at the AAMC home page on the Internet at http://www.aamc.org. The AAMC also provides in-depth information on medical education and other areas of interest to future physicians.

Association of American Medical Colleges
    2450 N Street NW
    Washington, DC 20037-1129
    202-828-0416
    www.aamc.org

Information on all aspects relating to a medical career is also easily available from the American Medical Association.

American Medical Association
  515 North State Street
  Chicago, IL 60610
  312-464-5000
  www.ama-assn.org

Council of Academic Societies members listed by discipline:

BASIC SCIENCES

Anatomy and Cell Biology

  American Association of Anatomists
  Association of Anatomy, Cell Biology, and Neurobiology
    Chairpersons

Biochemistry

  American Society for Biochemistry and Molecular Biology
  Association of Medical and Graduate Departments of
    Biochemistry

Microbiology

  American Society for Microbiology
  Association of Medical School Microbiology and Immu-
    nology Chairs

Neuroscience

  Society for Neuroscience

Pathology

    Academy of Clinical Laboratory Physicians and Scientists
    American Society for Investigative Pathology, Inc.
    Association of Pathology Chairs, Inc.
    U.S. and Canadian Academy of Pathology

Pharmacology

    American Society for Pharmacology and Experimental
      Therapeutics
    Association for Medical School Pharmacology

Physiology

    American Physiological Society
    Association of Chairmen of Departments of Physiology

CLINICAL SCIENCES

Anesthesiology

    Association of Anesthesiology Program Directors
    Association of University Anesthesiologists
    Society for Education in Anesthesia
    Society of Academic Anesthesiology Chairs

Dermatology

    Association of Professors of Dermatology

Emergency Medicine

Association of Academic Chairs of Emergency Medicine
Council of Emergency Medicine Residency Directors
Society for Academic Emergency Medicine

Endocrinology

Endocrine Society

Family Medicine

Association of Departments of Family Medicine
Association of Family Practice Residency Directors
Society of Teachers of Family Medicine

General Surgery

American Surgical Association
American Surgical Association Foundation
Association for Academic Surgery
Association for Surgical Education
Society for Surgery of the Alimentary Tract
Society of Surgical Chairmen
Society of University Surgeons

Genetics

American Society of Human Genetics

Internal Medicine

American College of Physicians
American Gastroenterological Association
American Society for Clinical Investigation

American Society of Clinical Oncology
American Society of Hematology
Association of American Physicians
Association of Professors of Cardiology
Association of Professors of Medicine
Association of Program Directors in Internal Medicine

Multispecialty

American Academy of Allergy, Asthma, and Immunology
American Geriatrics Society
American Society for Clinical Nutrition, Inc.

Neurology

American Academy of Neurology
American Neurological Association
Association of University Professors of Neurology

Neurosurgery

American Association of Neurological Surgeons

Obstetrics and Gynecology

American College of Obstetricians and Gynecologists
American Society for Reproductive Medicine
Association of Professors of Gynecology and Obstetrics
Council of University Chairs of Obstetrics and Gynecology
Society for Gynecologic Investigation

Ophthalmology

American Academy of Ophthalmology
Association of University Professors of Ophthalmology

Orthopaedics

   Academic Orthopaedic Society
   American Orthopaedic Association

Otolaryngology

   Association of Academic Departments of Otolaryngology—
     Head and Neck Surgery
   Society of University Otolaryngologists/Head and Neck
     Surgeons

Pediatrics

   Ambulatory Pediatric Association
   American Pediatric Society
   Association of Medical School Pediatric Department
     Chairmen
   Society for Pediatric Research

Pharmacology

   American College of Clinical Pharmacology
   American College of Neuropsychopharmacology
   American Society for Clinical Pharmacology and Thera-
     peutics

Physical Medicine and Rehabilitation

   American Academy of Physical Medicine and
     Rehabilitation
   Association of Academic Physiatrists

Plastic Surgery

American Association of Plastic Surgeons
Plastic Surgery Educational Foundation
Plastic Surgery Research Council

Preventive Medicine

Association of Teachers of Preventive Medicine

Psychiatry

American Association of Chairmen of Departments of Psychiatry
American Association of Directors of Psychiatric Residency Training
American College of Psychiatrists
American Psychiatric Association

Radiology

Association of University Radiologists
Society of Chairmen of Academic Radiology Departments

Thoracic Surgery

American Association for Thoracic Surgery
Graham Education and Research Foundation
Thoracic Surgery Directors Association

Urology

Society of University Urologists